"Why Won't the Landlord Take Visa?"

"Why Won't the Landlord Take Visa?"

The Princeton Review's Crash Course to Life After Graduation

By Tara Bray

Random House, Inc.
New York
www.randomhouse.com/princetonreview

Princeton Review Publishing, L. L. C.
2315 Broadway
New York, NY 10024
E-mail: comments@review.com

ISBN 0-375-76191-8

Editors: Erik Olson & Russell Kahn
Production Editor: Julieanna Lambert
Production Coordinator: Scott Harris

Manufactured in the United States of America.

9 8 7 6 5 4 3 2 1

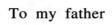

To my father

Acknowledgments

Thank you to all the people who helped in the writing of this book: Erik Olson and Russell Kahn at The Princeton Review; Rachel, Donna, Randy, and Elizabeth for their encouragement and suggestions; and all of the friends and family from whom I learned to survive. Their stories were my inspiration.

Thanks also to Julieanna Lambert and Scott Harris for their many hours spent shaping this text into a book.

Contents

Introduction

Stepping Up, Stepping Out

So you're degreed (or soon to be), legal, dispensing advice nostalgically to underclassmen, and have Big Plans for the future. Living with the parents is only an interim thing until Destiny comes knocking with a movie contract.

No dishes to wash. No bills to pay. Dad's Dodge Caravan. Mom's MasterCard. Home-cooked dinners every night. The mall's only a mile away, and Blockbuster is right around the corner. And after all, people in Spain live with their parents until they're thirty.

But are you cringing at those Holiday Inn commercials—the ones with Mom, Dad, Grandma, and one strangely familiar-looking hanger-on son or daughter—instead of laughing heartily? Are you feeling that you've got everything you need and you would be truly happy . . . if only Mom would stop ironing your T-shirts and making your bed when you're not in your room? And that *thing* that Dad does with his mouth at dinner. How did you live with it all those years? Then there's the issue with the phone, and your little brother who's addicted to Dragonslayer or whatever that game is that he plays over the Internet with some Swedish kid. And was your room always that small? And that poorly decorated? Those bunk beds were cool in fourth grade, but it feels weird having to decide each night: upper or lower?

You get the point. It's time to survive *without* your parents' money. But how?

Making it from college to the real world is about more than who pays the bills. It's about feeling comfortable on your own (or in an apartment you share with four people). It's about figuring out your destiny as well as your taxes, managing your goals in addition to your calendar.

In other words, surviving without your parents' money is about finding a balance between freedom and responsibility, and realizing that you can't have one without the other.

Maybe you started pizzaat2am.com in college, commanded a staff of forty, and are now ready to join the rest of the dot-com generation in San Francisco. You *still* need to know how to find an apartment in a city where you have to have a renter's resume.

Or maybe you're a fledgling writer/artist/digital diva. How do you keep yourself clothed, fed, and Starbucked while you're pursuing your dreams?

Even if the recent expiration of your student ID card is merely a temporary state of affairs (hurray for grad school!), why not actually have "life experiences" while you're writing about them for your entrance essays?

And for those of you who have never had the pleasure of paying an electric bill, cooking yourself a full meal, or sweet-talking a human resources officer into giving you an interview? This book should put you, the fledgling real-lifer (not to be confused with lifer, which requires a whole different set of skills, like soap carving and dictionary memorization), at ease.

Let's face it—despite what they say, your parents are actually terrified of you moving back in with them. You've developed awful habits since you left for college—like asserting your political opinions at the dinner table. Not to mention what you have to do to keep that belly-button ring clean!

So, even though unprecedented economic growth over the last decade might mean it's easier than ever to find a job, students and recent grads still could use some help navigating this brave new world.

All right, then. Buckle your seatbelt. Adjust your rearview mirror. Set your Global Positioning System to "Grownuphood." (We thought you'd like this better than Adulthood, which is full of scary things like annuities, golf, and baby showers.) Just don't forget to bring along your checkbook. Or your resume. Or your co-signer.

Co-signer? What's a co-signer?

Or this book. But we didn't have to tell you that.

CHAPTER 1

Mental and Emotional Preparation

Real World, Inc.

The real world? Isn't that a television program where a half-dozen or so people get to live together in a swank apartment in some cosmopolitan urban setting—New York, London, San Francisco—without paying rent? Isn't it where billions of people worldwide hang on your every decision, no matter how small or insignificant? Last *Real World* we saw, they had a pool with a volcano fountain in the middle, and they worried about keeping the camera out of the bathroom.

I'm a Star. I'm a Star. I'm a Big, Bright, Shining Star.
Think you got what it takes? For information about auditioning for *The Real World*, visit www.mtv.com/sendme.tin?page=/mtv/castingCall/&sub=shows.

THAT'S NOT THE REAL WORLD. Perhaps we should say this again: That's *not* the real world.

Even in our virtual reality of twenty-four-hour Web cams, dot-coms, and IPOs that seemingly make millionaires from a little HTML and some Javascript, *The Real World* is not the same as the plain old real world—which is, last time we checked, lowercase, copyright-free, and has no dot-anything at the end of it.

So let's just call it what it is—life. Your life, to be precise. You've been living it for a while now, and so far, you haven't needed a book to tell you how to do it (though *The Baby-Sitters Club* did have a few good suggestions). What's so different now?

Toto, We're Not in Iowa City Anymore (or Madison, or Eugene, or Chapel Hill).

It's called school, and soon it's going to be over—if it isn't already. (Remember that day you donned a cardboard cap and an ugly gown, sat in the sun for a few hours, went to brunch with your proud parents, and received unexpected checks from relatives in Michigan? *That* was graduation.) You might still be living in the same place—according to *American Demographics*, university towns are attracting more and more of the young, affluent, post-grad set—but admit it: those freshmen already look a lot younger than you. And once you're out, you're not going to fool anyone with the hat or the sweatshirt, buddy.

For some, the transition to the real world isn't hard—maybe they've been working part-time to put themselves through school; maybe their college town is New York or L.A. and they're used to the big, bad city. For others, the first months after the graduation kegs have been rolled away have left them unexpectedly bereft.

No matter how prepared you are to face the real world, the changeover is a little dizzying. College occupies a funny place in the American psyche: it offers all the freedom of adulthood (no parents, little supervision) without all the responsibility.

While this is all well and good when you're in the ivory tower, when it's all over . . . it's all over. Then what?

Breaking It Down: College vs. the Real World

So what exactly are the differences, you ask?

Say goodbye to . . .	*Say hello to . . .*
Earliest class at 11:00	7:30 A.M. status report meeting
Grabbing lunch after class with that hottie you met in Spanish	Having lunch at your desk while you try to avoid today's baby shower
The Quad	The Cubicle
Sweatpants 24-7	Casual Fridays
More friends than you can handle	Derek, the intern
Road trips and camping	Business travel and the Days Inn
Senioritis	Rookiedom
The sky's the limit	The glass ceiling
The credit card	The credit card bill
The keg	The water cooler
"Pete," your clog-wearing medieval lit. professor	"Liz," your cosmopolitan-swilling boss who dyes her twin French poodles to match her shoes
Furnished rooms	Futons and IKEA
Student loan agreements	Student loan payments
Sophocles	Spreadsheets

On the other hand, there are a *few* perks.

Say goodbye to . . .	*Say hello to . . .*
Cafeteria coffee	The daily double latte
Pizza parties	Client dinners
Tuition	Salary

All right, so the list is a bit tongue-in-cheek. Life after college is not all carpal tunnel syndrome and expense accounts. In fact, after a few years out, college will seem like a pleasant but hazy dream: heavy on exams, outdoor barbecues, and earnest late-night discussions. Time well spent, but you're glad it's over.

And despite the monotony of day-to-day life (photocopiers, commuting, and meetings are mostly unavoidable, whether you're a number cruncher on Wall Street or a beachboy in Miami), the world beyond those ivy-covered walls is deeply and infinitely interesting. That's hopefully what college—all those critical-thinking skills!—has helped you to realize: that life, like those bookshelves from IKEA, is a do-it-yourself kind of thing.

A B.A. and a Buck-Fifty . . .

. . . will get you a ride on the subway, or so the saying goes. But don't feel too bad; the same sentiment has been applied to everything from a law degree to a Ph.D. to a Master's in Fine Arts.

In reality, at least in terms of a career, the time has never been better for college grads. A decade ago, B.A.s were entering a job market packed with baby boomers at the height of their careers, but today those same baby boomers are starting to move into late-career positions, leaving entry-level work wide open for folks like you. And then there's the U.S. unemployment rate, which in May 2000 hit its lowest point in thirty years.

While we make no promises about the fate of the economy, steady growth in the United States throughout the 1990s and into the new millennium has meant higher and higher starting salaries—and more perks—for entry-level workers. Jobs in the tech industry lead the pack right now, but even in traditionally lower-paying fields like publishing, teaching, and nonprofit social services, starting wages are keeping up with a growing economy—and a growing need for skilled workers.

In fact, according to a survey conducted by the National Association of Colleges and Employers, more than half of college students had jobs by graduation day, 2000. Eighty percent were working within seven months. And while liberal arts majors started off at a lower salary ($29,000/year) than, say, your average computer engineer ($42,000/year), wages were up about 5 percent across the board from 1999.

It's Not Just a Job—It's an Adventure

Okay, so you know you'll probably find a job. If you went through your school's recruiting program, you might have one already. If you've never heard the term "career counselor," and would certainly not have wasted those last few months of quality partying time figuring out what it means, don't worry—we've got a few chapters for you.

But whether you're the gainfully employed type or an incorrigible layabout, the transition to the real world—we hope—is about more than just your job. It goes back to that whole "life" thing. You've been living it for a while now—what adventures, opportunities, and challenges is this new phase going to bring? How will you handle the transition from the fairly structured college environment to the more nebulous "working world"—where there are no majors, no dorms, and no special student status?

Movies for the Transition
Want some insight into what you want, or what you don't want, or what it'll be like if you have no idea where you're going? • *The Graduate* • *The Big Kahuna* • *St. Elmo's Fire* • *Reality Bites* • *Fandango* • *Good Will Hunting* • *Diner* • *Office Space* • *Kicking and Screaming* • *The Producers*

According to the Center for Career Services at Columbia University in New York City, making the transition from college to work "can be a daunting task. Breaking it down into a series of steps will enable you to manage the entire process." Here are a few things you can do to make the transition easier.

- **Rest and regroup.** Give yourself a little time after graduation, so that your decisions are based less on panic and more on planning. Take that trip across the country. Visit friends or relatives. Or just chill at home or at school with friends for a little while. A few months in an empty college town—or at home, for that matter—will be the best way to curb your procrastination about entering the real world.

- **Know yourself.** If you're the stay-at-home type, don't get on the next ferry to Alaska for the canning season. If you've been itching to get out of Burlington since you started college, don't hang around any longer than necessary. Do you see yourself in a urban setting? Semi-urban? Rural? If you grew up and went to college in Manhattan, it might be a secret dream of yours to live in a cabin in Montana, fly-fishing for a living. Go for it! Or say you're a farm girl from Iowa and would like to try your hand at single-in-the-city? Why not? We all have dreams. The first years after college are just the time to pursue some of them. Which means, of course, that you'll have to . . .

- **Risk it.** Go out on a limb! Follow your heart! They're clichés, but the very best kind. The truth is, you're young, you have energy and pluck, and no matter how many responsibilities you think you have now, *you don't have as many as you'll have later.* That's just the nature of getting older. So now's the time to try to make that crazy dream of yours of being a jazz musician/dot-com entrepreneur/photographer/organic farmer a reality. Careers have a way of getting hold of you (it might have something to do with a paycheck), and waiting to pursue a dream might mean that you never get a chance to fulfill it. This makes us bitter and prematurely ages us, and who wants that?

    Of course we're not advocating sinking your life savings into that little escargot stand by the sea you have always wanted to run. Following a dream takes planning, know-how, and time, and like everything else, you've got to start at the beginning. (In other words, you might want to rethink your "snail-on-a-stick" concept.) Plus, risk requires a high level of responsibility. Which brings us to . . .

- **Don't give your parents a heart attack.** Let your family know what you're doing and why. It will be good for you to clarify your plans, and good for their peace of mind. They just want information, not a signed contract telling them what you're going to do with the rest of your life.

And by the way, what is that?

CHAPTER 2

What You Want

Relax!

In deciding what you want to do with the rest of your life (i.e., what career you'd like, where you'd like to settle, whom you want to marry, what you'll name your children, whether you'll invest in a traditional or Roth IRA—you know, *the basics*), it's crucial that you remember one thing: *Relax!* There's no way you'll be able to choose what you want to do with the rest of your life right at this moment (life has a way of messing up the best-laid plans), so it's probably best that you stop trying.

Instead, use this transitional time to learn a little bit more about you, your goals, and how you see yourself evolving and working toward those goals over the next few years. Change, besides being a pain in the butt, allows us to learn something about ourselves—how we react to pressure, what we want out of life. It also helps us define our relationship with family and friends, thereby making us more independent, self-reliant, responsible . . . you know, all that good stuff.

"No More Mr. Nice Guy"

Schwarzenegger said it best, but here's a translation: When you're making your decisions about the coming years, *stop trying to please everyone.* You might think that this is a no-brainer, but you'd be surprised how much time you've already spent thinking about what other people want instead of what's best for Number One (that's you, by the way).

Want me to prove it to you? Fill in the blanks in the following sentences with words from your own life.

"_____ invites you to an interview only if your GPA is above _____."

"_____ only wants _____ majors."

"_____ says I have to move to _____."

Or how about these?

"_____ have made a lot of sacrifices for me."

"_____'ll kill me if I don't go to _____ school."

"_____ wants me to join the family _____ business."

Sound familiar? They're quotes from college seniors interviewed at their schools' career centers. (Proper nouns taken out to protect the innocent.) And most likely, you could have filled in the blanks with any number of people, places, and things. For instance, any of these sentences could have started with parents, professors, employers, "society," girlfriends, boyfriends . . . heck, even the dog might have wanted you to join the family wig-making business. As for required GPAs and majors, while benchmarks *are* important for certain professions, your most important characteristics are desire and passion. They'll go a long way in determining your eventual success or failure in any given job.

So what is it that *you* want?

"But wait!" you say. "I don't know yet. That's why I'm reading this chapter!" Okay, okay. When you're making a big decision, it's normal to consult as many sources of advice as possible. For some, that means parents, siblings, close friends, trusted mentors, even (*gasp!*) a how-to book like this one. For others, it's straight to the horoscope columns, the palm and tarot card readers, and the personality quizzes. While we favor good old Mom and Dad over the *Cosmo* "Bedside Astrologer," no one's advice is as pertinent to your future as your own wishes, and a little reflection in the early stages of your decision-making will go a long way.

But first, let's engage in some old-fashioned deconstruction—a slate-cleaning, as it were—so that we can better understand what larger forces are at work in your destiny.

What Your Parents Want

It's called the Family Agenda, and it usually sounds something like, "Honey, we only want what's best for you." Which means, of course:

- **They want you to be happy.** Being happy means being settled, with a dependable car, a solid job, and a retirement plan—movies on the weekends and a trip to Bermuda in the spring. Or, it could mean being a sign-waving civil rights lawyer in New York City, a macrobiotic yoga teacher in Boulder, or a continent-hopping investment banker. In any case, "happiness" bears an eerie resemblance to *their* lives—not necessarily your own.

- **They want complete financial and emotional security for you *right now*.** Never mind the fact that the entire employment landscape has changed from your parents' day. Flexibility, resiliency, speed, and creativity—these are the fundamental qualities of the "New Economy," according to former U.S. secretary of labor Robert B. Reich, writing in *Fast Company* magazine. This means young people entering the working world need to be able to finesse rapidly changing situations, bouncing back when things get tough. Hey, your parents, too, probably had moments of self-doubt, risk-taking, and perhaps even failure. But you're their beloved child! Only good things for you!

- **They don't want to have to worry about you anymore.** Remember those unexpected phone calls on Friday night when your dad just called "to chat"? They were actually checking up on you. (Why'd you think they called on the weekend?) Now that you're an adult, however, Mom and Pop actually *do* want to just chat. "Enough worrying, already!" they'll say. "He can make his own decisions on this one." And they'll be blissfully ready to stop advising you altogether, preferring the phrase "Well, I'm not going to tell you what to do anymore now that you're all grown up" rather than the dreaded (yet strangely comforting) "Dad and I think you should . . . ." At the same time, they'll be mortally wounded if you don't continue to share with them your deepest fears and problems (or call them every Sunday).

- **They want you to raise several children and be extraordinarily happy in your chosen career.** They just don't want to see you have to break a sweat doing it. Parents hate to see their children struggle—unless it's while you're raking the lawn.

- **They want to be able to brag about you.** Or at least they want to be able to out-brag that bigmouth Harry at the office, whose daughter just got her combined law degree/M.D./Ph.D. in bioethics.

- **They want you to not need them anymore.** Well, maybe just around the holidays. And on your birthday. And why don't you call anymore?

As you can see, the Family Agenda—while well intentioned—is a little conflicted. Sure, they want you to be a grownup, offering such gems as "Well, it's high time you start acting like one!" and "We thought we'd never see the day!" At the same time, they don't want to lose their baby. It's the age-old parental dilemma, and it's not going to be resolved anytime soon.

In the meantime, you have a life to live and, as you are well aware, some major decisions to make. Despite what you may have believed as an angst-filled teenager, your parents *do* understand you a little. That's why their advice seems so, well, *good*. To make things even more complicated, you might have a profession that runs in your family, or you may have grown up in a certain environment (e.g., academia or medicine) that you know intimately and with which you feel comfortable. In that case, the Family Agenda might become *your* agenda, which is perfectly natural, since you grew up in it.

What feels most comfortable and familiar, however, is not always what lets you grow and change, so make sure you spend at least a little time thinking about how your parents' desires could be consciously and unconsciously affecting your decisions. Remember, too, that "rebel" could also be a role that you've fallen into over the last few years.

Ultimately, parents really do want to see you happy—excited about your life choices, eager to enter the adult world. So they'll gripe and grumble a little if your true calling takes you to a tattoo studio in the East Village. The bottom line? They'll love you no matter what you choose.

What Your Friends Want

Friends, on the other hand, will not love you no matter what. That's why they're friends and not family. They are, however, the people whom you want to be around. And if you're like most people, some of your decisions in the coming years will be based on what your pals are doing. This isn't a bad idea—having a few friends around in a new situation can really soften a difficult transition. However, just like in grade school, it's important that you don't make your decisions just because "everybody's doing it." That was the point of the jumping-off-a-cliff story your dad told you in fourth grade. It still pertains today.

Instead, take stock of what your friends are doing; chances are you know a wide circle of people doing all sorts of things. Use them more as resources than advice-givers. So you have a pal in the Peace Corps in Senegal? Write to her and ask her what she loves and hates about the experience. A group of friends just moved to San Francisco to cash in on the dot-com revolution? Take a few weeks after school ends to visit them. Go on informational interviews, eat where they eat, hang out where they hang out. Ask them about their rent, the pros and cons of living in their neighborhood, and what it's like to work in a job where there might be little security but lots of excitement—and where the payoffs can be huge.

Consider yourself a free agent when it comes to your friends. Alas, even significant others fall into this category. Though we understand that the pull of your honey is great, if it's a strong relationship that's meant to last, a little distance and time won't change that. Plus, it will give you a chance to figure out some things on your own. For instance . . .

What You Want

If you're like most people, figuring out what movie to get at the video store is hard enough. Now we're asking you to decide something as important as your one and only life on earth! Oh, the pressure . . . the choices! It's positively paralyzing. Maybe you'll just go under the covers and take a nap. Surely it will all work itself out by the time you wake up . . . .

Unfortunately, a lot of people *do* go to sleep—at least figuratively—by moving where everyone else moves, taking a job through corporate recruiting that they thought would look good on their resume, and following the crowd instead of really considering where their heart is. Someday they'll wake up and ask themselves, "Where did all that time go?"

The truth is, as long as you stay awake—open to the world and its opportunities—and as long as you keep challenging yourself, it's hard to go wrong. That holds for softer stuff like where to live and whom to hang out with, as well as for harder choices like your future career and grad school. According to the Bureau of Labor Statistics, the average worker holds more than nine different jobs from ages eighteen to thirty-four. This humble writer alone held more than fifteen full-time positions in ten years—and lived to tell about it.

Everyone Needs a Little Philosophy

Books to get your head together . . . find yourself . . . lose yourself . . . figure out how to balance a checkbook (again):

- *Walden* by H. D. Thoreau
- *The Razor's Edge* by W. Somerset Maugham
- *Zen and the Art of Making a Living* by Laurence G. Boldt
- *Oh, the Places You'll Go!* by Dr. Seuss
- *The Nichomachean Ethics* by Aristotle
- *What Color Is Your Parachute?* by Richard Nelson Bolles
- *Wear Sunscreen* by Mary Schmich
- *The Unbearable Lightness of Being* by Milan Kundera
- The Bible
- The Koran
- Vedas

Each of those positions, however, moved me in the direction of becoming a professional writer. They also took me around the country, which broadened my perspective and gave me some great stories. Whether it was advertising or teaching English, proofreading or slinging sauerbraten at a German beer *haus*, each of my choices—whether I saw it at the time or not—helped me get where I am now.

Sure, there will be missteps along the way (telemarketing was one of mine), but remember: Stumbling around a little helps you learn what you *don't* want to do, which is almost (but not quite) as important as figuring out what you *do* want—narrowing your choices, so to speak.

Career Activism

Planning for the next few years? Throw out the old image of ladder climbing. (I was always afraid of heights, anyway.) Career counselor Barbara Moses, interviewed in *Fast Company* magazine, prefers the "career activist" model of employment. "Being an activist means that you stop, reflect, and look for meaning in everything you do," Moses says. In this model, there's room for more experimentation in different life modes (no long fall off the ladder), more flexibility, and more passion and creativity, *whatever* your profession. What matters is that your choices make sense to *you*.

So, as you start to make decisions about what to do next, consider *generally* what you would like to accomplish in the long term and *specifically* what you can do now to get there. Your ideas will change and become more specialized as you gain experience. What matters is that you look inside yourself to figure out what excites you. Who knows? An opportunity may arise somewhere down the line that you couldn't have predicted. Keeping yourself open and flexible about the particulars—while remembering your long-term goals—will open up experiences you might have never imagined possible.

You might even shift gears altogether. Susan, a managerial consultant at one of the top firms in Boston, decided she needed a little break in order to decide whether or not to go back to business school. She moved to Singapore, took a job as the managing director of an up-and-coming theater company, and used her skills to write press releases, fund-raise, and plan social events. While she did eventually decide to go back to grad school, returning to consulting once she got her M.B.A., she used her Singapore experience to tackle more arts-oriented assignments in her new job, advising entertainment-industry companies.

The First Step

So, you're *seriously* connected, you've got a lottery-winner's luck, and you're a prodigy/whiz kid/genius to boot. You found, the week after college, the job that you've always dreamed of at a rock-star salary. You're reading this book for its sheer literary value. We hate you. We hope your IPO fails.

Chances are, though, you're more like the rest of us, and need to start, well, *somewhere*. Maybe you've had a few jobs already, an internship or two during college, and a couple of ideas about where you might like to live for the next few years. You're flexible, but at the same time, you don't want to just take the first thing offered to you.

How about a little soul-searching? Refining your goals now can save you time spent looking through the classifieds later. Remember that your twenties, besides being a lot of fun, are also a time for figuring out who you are. The more self-reflection you do today, when you're relatively unencumbered, the less likely you'll be to wake up twenty years from now with a house, a mortgage, some rugrats, and a vague recollection of your youth. That's not to say you won't ever question yourself again. You will. You'll just get better at it as you go along.

Self-Assessment 101

Take out your resume. (If you don't have one, it's time to get one together. See chapter 10.) In lieu of a resume, or in addition to one, write down a list of the jobs and internships you've held over the last few years. Include any organizational, extracurricular, or fieldwork you've done (e.g., student council, drama clubs, educational trips), as well as any prizes, fellowships, or special honors you've garnered. Add any course work that you've felt particularly excited about. Finally, list what you perceive to be your "skills."

Do you have your own website? That means you know at least a little HTML. Spend a semester in Costa Rica? You can probably get by in conversational Spanish. Even skills you may take for granted—like being an awesome video-game player, being able to fix a car, or knowing Microsoft Office inside and out—are helpful here, as they can give you an idea of where your interests lie.

The point here is not to censor yourself. List as many of your skills and accomplishments as you can. Besides giving you an idea of where you may be headed, it's a great way to give yourself a confidence boost. You may have forgotten about that speech prize you won sophomore year, and how much pleasure it gave you to craft words into something that moved people.

Once you've brainstormed, review the list as if you were looking at someone else's life. Though it may seem counterintuitive, try to be as objective as you can here. What trends do you see? Do jobs, for instance, lead into one another, or are you all over the map? Have you made a few big changes recently (perhaps signifying a desire to change directions), or are you the slow and steady type, heading inexorably toward your ultimate goal? Try not to be judgmental; you've made each of your choices for a reason. Now you're just trying to decode what those reasons are and, from there, judge where you might want to go next.

Talent vs. Temperament

Making life choices is often a matter of finding where two things—your talent and your temperament—intersect. You may be a whiz with numbers but prefer the hallowed halls of academia to the big-money lifestyle of Wall Street. If that's the case, becoming a professor of economics may be much more rewarding than being a number cruncher in an investment banking firm, no matter how high the salary. Or maybe you're an art junkie and have great taste but you can't do without the finer things. Being an artist's representative may be a way to stay in the scene without having to forgo your beloved designer suits.

Talent

Discovering your talents may simply mean thinking about them. What are some of the things people have told you you're good at? Go back as far as you want to. Were you a crayon-wielding Picasso in elementary school? Write it down. Somebody besides your parents told you that you had an ear for music? Put that down, too. While going back through the years may not lead to earth-shattering revelations of your *metier* (as "profession" is known to the French), it may allow you to think more creatively about future plans.

Most important, however, is the list of talents *you* think you possess. Don't limit yourself to what you know right now. What might you be good at if you gave it a try? Oftentimes, what we think we're good at, or what we're interested in, are the things about which we're passionate. And when it comes down to it, passion goes a long way in determining how successful you'll be in any given job. If you love something, you'll be much more likely to want to spend a lot of time doing it (which, when it comes down to it, is the best definition of a career that we can think of).

Temperament

At least in this stage of your life, how you define your temperament will probably go a long way in determining how you want to spend the next few years. Where do you want to live? What kind of lifestyle do you want? Are you a "live to work" type, spending most of your available hours either at the office or hanging out with your business buddies, or do you work to live, scrimping and saving so that you can spend less time at work and more time enjoying yourself?

In some cases, what people do for recreation can also be their source of income, but even those folks who have "dream" jobs (actors, professional athletes, musicians) are usually notorious workaholics who have simply made their passion their profession. If you're the type who can't wait to get home at the end of the day so you can fool around with your video games, take heart. *There's nothing wrong with not being a workaholic.* In fact, it's downright healthy. However, you could also be a frustrated video game designer, in which case running home to your PlayStation could be a sign that you need both a career *and* a lifestyle change.

Where you want to live falls under this category as well. Depending on your job, you may not be able to pick exactly where you'll be for the next few years, but you should definitely spend some time thinking about what kind of environment you feel most comfortable in. City? Country? Suburbs? If you're an urban pioneer, what kind of city do you like? San Diego is very different from Detroit, though both are midsize cities. While this may seem obvious, folks will be different—as will the culture—depending on where you go. If you hate politics, D.C. may not be the best choice for you. Looking for a theater scene? If you're headed for L.A., make sure you're at least willing to do the film and TV thing, too.

Don't be afraid to look at smaller towns that may be very developed in a certain niche area. Iowa City, for example, has a fantastic writing scene, partially because of its well-known Iowa Writers' Workshop. And Sun Valley, Idaho, is a kind of nexus for serious outdoor types, drawing river-rafting guides, fly-fishing aficionados, skiers, and serious hikers from all around the country. Detroit's supposed to be down with the electronica/rave/trip hop scene, while Asheville, North Carolina, is the place to go if you're the mellow folksy/artsy fiddle-and-banjo type. Madison, Wisconsin, is known for its progressive politics and civic-mindedness; Portland, Oregon, for its plethora of tech jobs. The list goes on.

Just Gimme the Cash

Finally, there's the whole issue of money. One of the hardest aspects of decision-making is finance. But while there are certain differences between professions (nonprofit work may never allow you to buy that private jet you've been coveting), if financial comfort is important to you, you'll probably seek it out in whatever profession you're in. It's one of those talent vs. temperament things; you just can't get away from it. And while we all like to feel at least a modicum of financial stability, if money's your primary concern, make your decisions accordingly.

No matter where your mind's at in this matter, trust in the universe. If you follow your passion, you'll most likely be good at what you do. Being good at something usually means being compensated fairly. Of course, you could be a misunderstood genius, in which case you'll need this book even more than you thought you did.

CHAPTER 3

Helter Shelter

Some will argue about the basics of survival—listing, for example, food before shelter, or clothing before both. (I can't *live* without my Manolo Blahniks!) Considering the plethora of options for cheap and healthy food (see chapter 4), and considering that by this time you can probably dress yourself, the first thing we need to do is get you housed. That way you'll have a home base from which to carry out your world domination schemes. Or, at the very least, you'll have somewhere besides a park bench to crash.

The Commandments of Living on Your Own

After college, my boyfriend and I decided to move to Portland, Oregon, from the East Coast. I had no good reason, mind you. Probably I had heard something about Portland being a great place to live, with lots of hiking and cheap rent. Neither of us had a job. Nor did we have a place to live. Nor did we have any friends in Portland.

It was what I consider a worst-case scenario: with all our belongings packed into his powder-blue diesel Rabbit, we cruised in on Labor Day, one of the busiest traveling weekends of the year. All of the cheap motels were full. Even some of the not-so-cheap motels were full. Determined to survive on our own, my boyfriend and I spent the next week camping out with loggers and wayward churchgoers (there was a Bible camp down the street) across the Columbia River in Vancouver, Washington. We trekked into Portland each morning—a little rough around the edges from sleeping in a tent in the rain—to find an apartment and try to land jobs.

We finally found both, and everything worked out okay, but it illustrates the first commandment of living on your own. . . .

Thou Shalt Make Prior Arrangements (or at Least Pack a Tent)

If you're moving somewhere without an apartment, get yourself a place to stay. Give yourself at least a month or two if you're trying to find a place in a large urban area, making sure the place where you're staying is safe and that you have enough room to have some peace of mind while you carry out your search. (This means you cannot sleep in the bathtub.) Arrange with your host to pay part of the rent. Discuss this in advance and write it out on paper. While this may not be a binding contract, it will help fix a sum—and the duration of your stay—in everyone's mind.

While you're staying with folks, be overly helpful and extra neat. Offer to do the dishes, and fix that leaky faucet if you're handy. When you leave, buy them something useful—a nice juice pitcher, a martini shaker set, grapefruit spoons, whatever. It's the thought that counts, and it will *definitely* be appreciated.

Besides staying with friends, there are a few short-term alternatives that can help you bide some time while you look for a place.

- Every town with a university will have students who leave for summer, as well as faculty and grad students who go on leave. You can sublet their dorm rooms or apartments for a month or two to conduct your apartment and job search without inconveniencing your friends. Check bulletin boards in the university's student center, bus shelters, and the like. Contact someone at the student housing office and ask about university sublets. The student housing office of Columbia University in New York City, for example, has so many sublets that they've created an online search service for listings: www.aptzone.com.

- Motels, while expensive, can tide you over in the short term. This is an especially good option if you're moving with friends, which can help defray the costs. Don't compromise safety in order to save a few bucks; stay in recognized national chains in a well-lit, safe area.

- A last resort, as my little story illustrates, is always camping. Obviously, this is only an option if you are moving to a smaller town (New York City's camping isn't recommended). Choose a state or federal camp ground that has bathroom facilities, hot showers, and preferably a campsite manager. Private campgrounds might be cheaper, but tend to attract the trailer set. *Do not, under any circumstances, camp alone.* If you're by yourself, opt for a motel for the few extra bucks.

Thou Shalt Budget (at Least) a Month

No matter how sure you are about your girlfriend's cousin's best friend's phat pad right on the ocean, you'll need at least a month before you can actually move into your own place. Remember that searching takes a while. So does checking credit and references. So does clearing your check for the first month's rent and security deposit. So does the move-in process. In cities like San Francisco and New York, where the housing market is legendarily tight, budget two months. You'll need it.

Thou Shalt Be Prepared

Before you start your housing search in earnest, there are a few things you can do to take some of the heartache out of apartment hunting. Between looking in the classifieds, trolling the streets for FOR RENT signs, and going to open houses, finding a place can be a full-time occupation (for which you are not getting paid). Minimize the pain with a little planning.

If you're new to a place and don't have a phone, get a cell phone or a beeper, or set up a private voicemail box. Calls often come at the last minute. At that point, it doesn't matter where you are on the application waiting list—the person who signs the lease first gets the apartment.

If you've never signed a lease before, you'll probably need a co-signer. (A co-signer is a person who jointly signs a contractual agreement along with you. Their signature guarantees that in case you default, they will fulfill the contractual obligations of the lease.) This also goes for those of you who may have lived in previous apartments but don't yet have a monthly income. Your parents or guardians are usually the best bet for a co-signer, but ask their permission to use them before you sign anything.

Make sure your credit is good. Landlords will take a day or two to check your credit history, and they'll reject your application if your credit is bad. If you have any reason to question the soundness of your credit (late credit card, phone, or student loan payments, for example), you can request a copy of your credit history from Trans Union (800-888-4213) or Equifax (800-997-2493) for a nominal fee. If you have credit problems, don't try to hide them. Talk to your landlord and offer to have the lease co-signed.

In San Francisco, where rents have gone through the roof and hundreds of people at a time show up for apartment showings, a renter's resume is mandatory. While this may not be necessary in other places, you will have to fill out a renter's application. Besides providing all the information for those application forms, attaching a renter's resume to your application shows that you're organized and forthright with your rental history, traits that a prospective landlord will appreciate. And hey, it's *classy*.

What's on a renter's resume? Following pretty much the same format as an employment resume, a renter's resume should include such information as:

- Your name, social security number, and contact information

- Rental history (addresses, dates of residence, landlords' contact information)

- Employment history (your last two or three jobs is sufficient, with salary range and contact information)

- Personal references (names and contact information of three adults who will vouch for your character)

- Your bank's name and contact information, along with your checking/savings account number

Thou Shalt Know Thy Market

First, what's your budget? As a rule of thumb, your rent should be between one and two weeks' worth of net salary. Don't get in over your head here. Eviction is simply no fun.

It's also important that what you want matches what's out there. That means looking in the papers, asking friends, and generally getting as much information about the place you are moving to as possible. What are the rents in which areas? What can you expect to pay, for example, for a two-bedroom share in Lakeview in Chicago? A studio apartment in New Orleans? A 1950s bungalow in West Hollywood?

And there's more: How do most landlords in your chosen location list their properties? In New York, the majority of available spaces are listed with brokers, who charge a fee (approximately one month's rent, though it can be significantly higher) for their services. In Chicago, the top rental properties are listed in the *Chicago Reader*, which also has an online service called SpaceFinder (www.chireader.com). In some cities, your best bet is to simply walk down the streets of the neighborhood you're interested in, ringing up superintendents and taking down numbers along the way.

Furthermore, you'll need to find out what the lingo is in your city's real estate listings. "Prewar" may not mean anything to you, but in New York, it's shorthand for buildings constructed before World War II, which usually offer more square footage, nice architectural details (hardwood floors, moldings), and a heftier price tag. Familiarize yourself with the abbreviations used for classified listings so you'll know what you're getting.

It also helps to know the protocol for renting in your new city (e.g., aspects like the renter's resume, brokers, signing on the spot, etc.). Make sure you know the drill before you go to your appointments. Also, a city is often dominated by a certain kind of apartment building. Chicago, for example, is mostly three- or four-flat brownstones. San Francisco has a lot of duplexed Victorians. In Houston you're likely to live in an apartment or condominium complex complete with pool and Jacuzzi. New York's apartments have been reconfigured so many times you never know what you may get.

The point is, don't hold out for that perfect SoHo loft if you're moving to Tulsa. At the same time, you will probably *not* find an all-weather rooftop tennis court if you're going to make your home in, say, Juneau.

Finally, different neighborhoods have very different characters. Don't expect a plethora of hip coffee shops and swanky boutiques in an area inhabited mostly by working-class families. At the same time, so-called "gentrified" neighborhoods may have nice shops but, because of their transient population, may lack a sense of community. Make sure you know and feel comfortable with the area in which you're looking.

Top Ten Places to Live
Best Place to Get Lost: Homer, Alaska
Get Found: Charlottesville, Virginia
Have It Both Ways: Santa Cruz, California
Start a Business: Portland, Oregon
Stake Your Claim: Franconia, New Hampshire
Live Without Shoes: Hana, Hawaii
Raise a Family: Ann Arbor, Michigan
Become an Überjock: Boulder, Colorado
Learn a Language: St. Martin/Sint Maarten
Become an Old Salt: Portland, Maine

(Source: *Outside* magazine, May 1999)

Thou Shalt Know Thy Taste

Know what you're looking for in a domicile. How about a 3BR, $2\frac{1}{2}$BA w/fpl, hdwd fl, huge kit, A/C, w/d?

Huh?

In apartment-speak, that's a three-bedroom, two-and-a-half bath apartment with a fireplace, a huge kitchen, hardwood floors, air conditioning, and a washer/dryer. It may seem obvious, but a home is more than just a collection of abbreviations. It's your solace—the place that you like to come back to, the place where you entertain, laze around in the mornings, play your music loud, do your yoga . . . whatever it is you're into.

In an ideal world this would be easy. In the real world, flexibility is key. So on your quest for the perfect pad, you'll probably be forced to make a few compromises. Is space more important than privacy? If so, sharing a two- or three-bedroom apartment may be better than cramming yourself and the contents of your eighteen-foot U-Haul into a tiny studio. Would you be willing to pay less and compromise sunlight (and, sometimes, safety) for a garden- or basement-level apartment? For some, a dark apartment equals certain depression. If you're one of those folks, don't be fooled into thinking that you'll be just fine down there in Hobbitland. Opt for an apartment on the upper floors. Have special needs? Most buildings are required by law to be handicap-accessible, but before you trek out to look at it, get all the pertinent information from the broker or landlord.

First things first: Make a cheat sheet of things your ideal apartment would have, in order of preference. You'll have to do without the better part of your list, but at least you'll have a decent idea of what you're looking for when you start searching.

Thou Shalt Consult the Classifieds (and Online Listings and Bus Shelters and Telephone Poles)

So you've gotten your renter's resume together. You know you want a studio or one-bedroom apartment with lots of light on the third or fourth floor of a brownstone. And you're willing to compromise on the rest. You've checked out minimum and maximum rents in the areas you're looking in, as well as the types of units that are most likely to be available. This has already been the most time-consuming thing you've ever done in your entire life, and there's more? Yes. You've actually got to find the place.

There are several sources for apartments, each a little bit different. Try one or all—something's bound to turn up.

- **Word of mouth:** The best apartments often never make it to the classifieds. Either their occupants know what a good deal they have and never leave, or the apartment gets leased the old-fashioned way: by word of mouth. The first thing you do when you're looking to move? Ask everyone you know whether they know of an apartment for rent.

- **Traditional classifieds:** This includes a city's main newspapers, as well as its alternative weeklies and real estate rags. While the *Honolulu Advertiser* might carry all the apartment listings you'll need in that city, *The New York Times* most definitely will not. (In New York, check out *The Village Voice*.) In Chicago, both the city's biggest newspapers (the *Sun-Times* and the *Tribune*) carry rentals, but you're more likely to find what you're looking for in the young-person-friendly *Reader*. Real estate classified listings are usually reserved for selling and buying, but you never know what might turn up.

- **Online classifieds:** This includes the Web versions of what appears in the newspaper, usually searchable by type of apartment and price range. These usually show up before the hard copy is printed, so look here first for up-to-the-minute information. There are also online classifieds that carry Web-only listings. Try national real estate sites such as www.rent.net, www.homestore.com, and www.apartmentsearch.com.

- **FOR RENT signs:** Try to take at least one or two weekday mornings (it will give you an edge over the competition) to stroll through the neighborhoods you like. Look on front lawns, front doors, and first-floor windows. You can often buzz the apartment manager or super and look at the place right then. Plus, all that walking is the best thing you can do to get to know a neighborhood.

- **Bulletin boards, bus shelters, telephone poles, and other low-tech listing services:** Before the Net, a bulletin board was the extent of a neighborhood's "community space." They still exist in coffee shops, university student centers, libraries, and grocery, record, and bookstores. These are especially good places to look for apartment shares, sublets, and cooperative housing, as well as more casual arrangements that may or may not require a lease.

Thou Shalt Acknowledge That Sharing is a Virtue

You may already be planning to move in with friends, both for company and to cut costs. If you don't know anyone but are still interested in finding a share, there are lots of ways to find a prospective roommate. Ask around, then check the alternative weeklies, the bulletin boards, and the bus shelters, just as if you were looking for a place for yourself. Some cities even have apartment sharing services, either online or in the phone book. Try www.roommateaccess.com or www.roommatelocator.com.

While a little less private, co-ops and other community living situations offer a very social atmosphere for not much dough. Living conditions range from private rooms with separate food areas to loft spaces with communal kitchens. And though co-ops are found most often in towns with lots of alterna-people, like Eugene, Oregon, and Northampton, Massachusetts, they're springing up in cities, too, as a stand against the higher costs of urban living. You can get information about cooperative housing from the National Cooperative Business Association at www.cooperative.org, or from the National Association of Housing Cooperatives at www.coophousing.org.

Living for Free?

Don't want to spend *anything* on your rent? Domestic positions—which include everything from nannies and au pairs to nurses, housekeepers, cooks, gardeners, and caretakers—will usually provide you with a salary as well as a place to live. Berths can vary wildly, however—from separate bachelor apartments to the room right next to the baby's nursery—as can the amount of work and "free" private time. Don't get yourself into a situation you can't handle. Make sure you're willing to compromise your privacy, no matter what they say about a separate entrance.

Thy Broker Is Thy Friend

Essentially, a broker does your legwork for you—searches classifieds, checks out suitable spots, and culls only the types of apartment for which you're looking. So, if it's high ceilings, hardwood floors, exposed brick, and a clawfoot tub you're after, a broker will most definitely say, "No problem!" All for a fee, of course.

A broker's fee can range from a few hundred dollars to several thousand, depending on the monthly rent. Standard fees range from 100 to 150 percent of a full month's rent. This money, unlike your security deposit, does *not* get refunded to you at the end of your lease, so before using a broker, make sure you really and truly need one.

In certain cities where the rental market is legendarily tight, a broker is almost mandatory for finding a place. In fact, many available units in the Big Apple don't even get listed in the papers. Landlords head straight for a broker, who will also screen tenants, weeding out possible problems.

Thou Shalt Know Thy Basics

So you've done your research, found a few places, and made some appointments. Now you're going to get a chance to look at some apartments. *Hallelujah!* Though it will be tempting to take the first place you see because of sheer exhaustion, the most important part of the process—and the one most overlooked—is this: No matter how much the manager/landlord/broker tries to rush you through her twenty-seventh viewing that day, take your time and check the place out.

- **Rent:** How much is it? What's the security deposit? What's included? Water? Gas? Heat? Electricity? Cable? Free *New York Times* delivery? Doubtful. And while you lucked out if you found a place with a pool or hot tub, prepare yourself for *very* high water and electricity bills, as well the cost of a "pool guy" (or gal) once a month.

- **Locks/Deadbolts:** Are they on all the doors, including the outer door?

- **Intercom:** Does it work?

- **Windows:** Do they open, close, and lock? If you're in the city, make sure there are grates on all windows that are accessible from the ground. Ask about insulation for windows during winter.

- **Fire escape:** It's unlawful for a building higher than a few stories not to have a fire escape or some other kind of fireproof exit. Make sure yours is in good condition.

- **Heat: electric, central, or radiator?** Remember, electric heat is very expensive. If you're up north and have electric heat, expect hundreds of dollars on your electric bill during the winter months.

- **A/C:** Air conditioning made the South livable, or so they say. If you're counting on your A/C to keep you comfortable in the hot months, be sure it cools down more than just the few feet of space around the window.

- **Water quality, pressure, and temperature:** Is it drinkable? Can you brush your teeth with it? As for water pressure and heating, older city buildings are notoriously bad on both counts. Usually no amount of complaining to the landlord will change the situation. If long, hot showers are important to you, find another place.

- **Working toilets:** How old is the plumbing? If you're living with a few people, this question suddenly becomes very, shall we say, *urgent*.

- **Working fridge, stove, and oven:** Is the stove gas or electric? If it's gas, locate the pilot light. If it doesn't light automatically, have your landlord show you how to light the stove. Gas can be very dangerous if not handled properly.

- **Smoke detectors and fire extinguishers:** Not all buildings have these. If you're concerned about fire safety, ask your landlord to install one or both.

- **Electrical outlets:** Make sure you've got plenty of the three-pronged electric outlets—older buildings, especially, have very few. Be wary of jury-rigged wires—they can cause fires.

- **Phone jacks:** If there's not one in every room, check for sufficient jacks for every resident *and* their computer. If there aren't enough jacks and you really love the apartment, consider spending a little extra to install a DSL or ISDN line. Find out if a cable modem is available for the place.

- **Creepy-crawlies:** Even the most charming apartments can be rodent-infested roach motels underneath the shiny facade. Check in cabinets, around woodwork (foundations if you're looking at a house), and under kitchen appliances for telltale droppings, dead bugs, and/or one too many pest traps.

- **Finally, check for damage:** (See Thou Shalt Read Thy Lease on page 29 for more on this.) Check for wall scuffs and carpet stains, cracks in the shower and leaky faucets. Turn everything on and off a few times, and don't be afraid to look under cabinets, behind doors, and under furniture. Landlords may occasionally lower the rent for you if the place has something really wrong with it, like not enough water pressure to drown an ant. You can also offer to fix a few things for lower rent. But don't get in over your head here; often, the clearer your tenant/landlord boundaries, the better your relationship.

Thou Shalt Consider the Finer Things

- **Higher equals hotter:** In older buildings especially, the top floors get all the heat from the floors below. If you can control your heat from inside your apartment, a higher floor may mean a little less on heating bills during the winter.

- **Major appliances:** If there's no washer/dryer in the apartment or in the building's laundry room, is there a Laundromat nearby? Nobody likes to carry their clothes several blocks to wash them. Some buildings have washers with no dryers. Make sure you're cool with wet laundry hanging in the bathroom. A dishwasher may be a friendship-saver if you're sharing a place with a bunch of folks. If you're not, it's nice but not necessary.

- **Lighting:** Don't let the 1970s chandelier fool you. Older apartments need lots of standing lamps, an added expense.

- **Floors:** Almost everyone prefers hardwood floors over carpet, which shows stains and holds on to the odors of former tenants— like Midge, the ninety-year-old cigar-smoking Chihuahua breeder. Because of this, landlords are *very* protective of their floors and may require you to cover every inch with (expensive) throw rugs.

- **Changing the apartment:** Can you cover the cornflower-blue heart stencils in the kitchen? Tear down the Garfield wallpaper in the bedroom? Rip out the shag? Can you build a sleeping loft? Some landlords are flexible in these areas, even offering a discount on the rent for rehabbing. Again, tread carefully in these waters before you get in over your head.

- **The condition of the grounds and common spaces:** Even if the inside of the apartment is nice, check out the surrounding areas. This usually tells you how good the landlord/super is at keeping up the place.

- **Pets:** First, a public service announcement brought to you by the Association to Stop People from Thinking Pets Are Stuffed Animals: Getting a pet right after college, no matter how much you want one, and how much you think it will make you feel magically "settled" is a good idea *only if you are sure you will be able to house and care for it for the next twenty years of your life.* If you are sure, then you may ask the landlord whether he or she accepts pets.

- **The building's outdoor spaces:** Find out the rules concerning the building's roof, pool, or deck. A rooftop view can be a priceless perk, but it's no good paying for it if you can't use it.

- **Elevator/Stairs:** Move-in day without an elevator is *no fun at all*. A five-story walk-up can get very annoying very quickly, and you should take that into account with the price of rent.

- **Car:** If you have a car, is parking included? Extra? Impossible to find? Do you need a city permit?

- **Finally, the landlord/super:** Be sure the people that you'll be dealing with for the next . . . well, however long . . . are sufficiently fair and responsive. My first landlady was neither. An eighty-three-year-old, amply endowed Romanian who spoke very little English, she'd sit on the back porch in her underwear during the summer and complain about her diabetes. Fortunately, she was an amazing storyteller and quite a character, which made up for the fact that I had to sweep the hall every month. The point is, there are many different types of landlords. Should yours be a stinker, look for the bright side. If there isn't one, look for another place.

Thou Shalt Read Thy Lease

The moment has arrived. Your application has gone through, your credit has been checked, you've got the first month's rent and security deposit (check or money order) in one hand and a pen in the other. It's either sign this lease now or move home to Mom and Dad permanently so you'll never have to think about toilets, fire extinguishers, wallpaper, and pool guys again.

Whoa! Just like you took the time to look over your apartment, you'll need to read your lease carefully before you sign it. While the following list doesn't take into account every type of lease there is, a standard rental lease will cover:

- **Terms of the lease:** Its start and end date, policies for subletting, and obligations of landlord, signer, and co-signer in case of a lease-breaking.

- **Security deposit:** How much, and what the stipulations are for having the entire amount refunded to you at the end of your stay. (This might mean a spic-and-span apartment with no damage, or a place that's "broom clean" with minor wall scuffs, etc. It all depends on your landlord.)

- **Rent payments:** To whom, by what date, in what form, and what the fee is for late payments.

- **List of damage:** Before you sign, go through the apartment, noting any damage. This will be part of your lease, and your proof against any attempt to withhold part of your security deposit later.

Thou Shalt Have Utilities (and Pay for Them)

Thought the lights just magically come on when you want them? And phone service appears, ready to take your calls, when you first lift the receiver? Wrong. Electricity, heat, water, phone, and cable are called *utilities*—just think of the faucet on the Monopoly board—and they cost money. They also require you to arrange for hookup. Here's a guide to some of your favorites.

- **Water:** Most places pay for water. If yours doesn't, ask why. Your water should be on already when you move in to the place.

- **Heat:** Some places pay for heating, too. If not, and you have gas heat, call the gas company in your area. Service usually takes a few days to a week to get hooked up. If you're moving in during the winter, the heat is probably already on to prevent your pipes from freezing. You just need to transfer the account to your name. It's illegal for gas companies to turn your heat off in winter, even if you fail to pay your bill—which, of course, we do not suggest. This book is about *survival,* after all.

  Also find out about the cooking gas, which probably comes from the same company that supplies your heat. Ask how much these bills tend to be, since they can be quite significant.

- **Electricity:** Ask your landlord what the local electric utility is in your area, and set up service. In most cases, your electric provider can have only one person responsible for the account. This means one person will have to be responsible for getting reimbursed from his or her roommates.

- **Phone:** This is the mother of all utilities. The possibilities for phone service are endless. With deregulation, certain national companies can now provide local service. And that doesn't even start to take into account all the long-distance services, 1010 numbers, second lines, broadband (DSL and ISDN), voicemail, call waiting, and caller ID options out there. Before you sample the many delights of telecommunications, however, you'll need basic local service, which will run you about fifty dollars for setup, plus another thirty to fifty dollars for the basic monthly cost of having a line. If you've never had an account before, you may also have to set down a deposit of a few hundred bucks, just in case.

Remember, this is all *before* you start making any calls. As with the electric service, phone accounts can usually have only one bill. Unlike electricity, however, phone service can take *weeks* to get set up. Order service as soon as you sign a lease by calling your local phone company. If you're concerned about sharing your phone with a roommate, suggest that you split the cost of installing another line. Another option, depending on your phone company, is setting up dialing codes for long-distance calls. A final option is to get rid of your land line altogether, opting for a high-speed digital line (or digital cable) for your computer and a cell phone for voice calls.

- **ISP:** Remember that you're not on campus anymore—you'll need an Internet Service Provider in order to log on. There's no shortage of them out there, and both national and local ISPs can provide you with the access you need. Just make sure you've got a plan that works with your tastes, your speed requirements, and your budget. Some sites offer free dial-up for users, though you've got to withstand a daily onslaught of advertising to get it. Try free nationwide ISPs such as DotNow.com, NetZero.com, and Tritium.net.

Thou Shalt Have Furnishings

From the ages of twenty to twenty-six, I moved *every year*. That's right, for six years straight, every spring I'd pack up all my belongings in boxes and garbage bags and haul them to the next spot. You'd think I'd have become something of a minimalist—quite the contrary! I call it the "bag-lady syndrome," as vagabonding actually *increases* your propensity for junk. When I finally cleaned everything out, I realized I'd been carting around the most ridiculous stuff: old yogurt containers and half-empty cleaning supplies, broken computer components, clothes too big or too small or too ugly, wrong-size sheets, weird bits of broken glass and feathers and river rocks. If it was useless, I was sure to pack it carefully into boxes and move it to the next destination. I guess it made it feel like home.

Wherever you fall on the maximalist–minimalist spectrum, the difference between a regular old *house* (or apartment, or trailer, or old school bus, or wherever you hang your hat) and a *home* is what you put in it. (That includes you, of course!) In other words, *home* is not made by certain well-known Swedish furniture manufacturers, nor does it come in a box, nor are there step-by-step instructions for its assembly. Making your humble abode into a creative reflection of your taste and personality takes time and energy . . . and it's fun!

Move-In

Bribe your friends with pizza and unlimited beer. Blast the music (respecting your new neighbors, of course), and promise a party after the sweaty stuff is over. If you have no friends . . . well, see chapter 6, and in the meantime, look around on bulletin boards and bus shelters for movers in your area. You can usually get a few people to help you for as little as twenty dollars an hour.

Necessities

Give the place a good old-fashioned spring cleaning—*before* you unpack. Once the furniture gets moved in, certain areas of your apartment disappear forever.

Don't have anything to sleep on? Well, there's always the ubiquitous futon, available for about $300 more than you'll be able to sell it for in two years when you decide you want a real bed. (If you're looking for a used futon, proceed with caution. Futon mattresses wear poorly if they aren't taken care of.) Whether you're going the futon route or opting for a regular mattress, look for a used bed first. Prices are about ten times less than what a new bed goes for, and often, people are so hot to get rid of the thing that they'll deliver it for free. If you want to go new, several retailers offer free delivery. Then there's always the provocatively named Dial-a-Mattress, available in most major urban areas.

The Tao of Home Furnishing

We recognize that empty apartments are depressing. If you must make a trip to the local superstore, avoid the desire to fill your place up all at once. Just get your basics: something to sit on, something to eat on, something to hold your books, and something to hold your computer. This allows you the freedom to get creative with your space, on the cheap or *free*! How, you ask? *Simple.*

Develop a style. This is the most important lesson. Until you have a style of your own, you'll buy whatever the advertisers tell you is cool, which will be hopelessly out of date in about three years. The Tao of home furnishing gently urges us away from uniformity and toward individuality, away from gloss and glitz and toward things with character (if maybe a few scratches and dents). Organize your style around themes or colors you like, and don't be afraid of mixing and matching. Six beautiful china plates in different, but complementary, patterns is much cooler (and less expensive) than an el cheapo set.

Likewise, broaden your idea of what you consider art. While posters of favorite paintings and rock stars are fine, consider other objects of beauty to hang on your walls: early-1960s record covers, wooden alphabet blocks, old signs, homemade assemblages (three-dimensional collages—think of those dioramas from grade school and you're on the right track), thrift store art, even vintage clothes can be tacked up and called art. If the Modernists did it with urinals, so can you.

Dumpster Dive

This is not actually as pungent as it sounds. Most people, when they're too lazy to take their stuff to the thrift store, just set it in their alleys, or on their stoops or sidewalks, neatly piled up next to the *real* trash. In other words, they *want* you to take it. In addition to large items of furniture, I've found a Cuisinart, vintage 1950s fabric, a turntable, a six-foot bamboo blind, and other nifties too numerous to list here. Best time to troll the streets? Move-out days and, in college towns, Labor Day or around graduation.

> **Best Places to Live**
>
> **Big City:**
> San Francisco, California
> Austin, Texas
> New York, New York
>
> **Small City:**
> Rochester, Minnesota
> Boulder, Colorado
> Columbia, Missouri
>
> (Source: Money.com, 2000)

Frequent garage, yard, stoop, tag, house, and apartment sales. Here you can find truly *excellent* stuff. Look in the usual places for listings. Make sure to bicker. When you get good at it and accumulate enough stuff, you can have your own sale. You'd be surprised at what people buy. (These are also great places to buy art supplies, which can be expensive new.)

Rummage at thrift stores. Not good for underwear, but great for pretty 100 percent–cotton pillowcases and sheets, kitchen supplies (the two-dollar toaster), doodads of various kitschy tastes, old books and records, bizarre art, vases, you name it. Look for green-tag days and the like when things can get *really* cheap.

Scan the classifieds. If there's a big-ticket item like a stereo, TV, or VCR you're vying for, look at the classifieds, "penny saver" papers, and online sites first (eBay.com, Loot.com). You'll get high quality for a fraction of the retail cost.

Cleanliness Is Next to Godliness

Or so the saying goes. But we'd like to amend it a little bit. Cleanliness is next to impossible unless you put your mind to it. Those stupid roommate cleaning wheels never work—though they do provide hours of laughter and entertainment for bemused guests. If everyone in the house likes cleaning, great. If not, save yourself needless arguing by hiring a housecleaner to come in once in a while—especially on move-in and move-out days or after parties. Cleaning services go from ten dollars an hour and up, plus a tip.

Respect Thy Neighbor (Until She Breaks Your Stereo)

This goes for apartment shares as well as the folks that live down the hall. If you've lived in a dorm, you know how important it is to respect a person's privacy and quiet. Besides that, it's just good sense. Wash your dishes, keep the common spaces neat, and if you're having people over, let your roomie know.

A little courtesy goes a long way, especially with landlords, doormen, supers, and apartment maintenance workers. A bottle of wine or a nice tip around Christmas lets people know you appreciate their help, and increases the likelihood of getting that leaky faucet fixed next time you call.

Should there be problems, remember that notes with lots of exclamation marks only go so far. You'll have to talk about it at some point, and the sooner the better. If a living situation just isn't working, break your lease or find a subletter and move out. The more protracted a disagreement, the uglier it can get, and that just isn't worth the hassle.

Thou Shalt Remember the Little Things

A few final reminders of the miscellaneous sort:

- Leave a set of keys with a friend, just in case you get locked out.

- Take your trash out every few days, unless you like roaches and rats.

- And finally, buy a good knife, a few quality tools, an old-fashioned rag mop, and some Murphy's Oil Soap (because it makes your apartment smell good).

The rest? You're on your own, boys and girls. Well, at least until the next chapter.

CHAPTER 4

Good Food

If you're like most folks right out of college, your culinary expertise is probably limited to the basics (fried eggs, ramen, pasta with red sauce, and macaroni and cheese), as well as a dish or two that you probably learned from home. In your new independent life, you're determined to save money and cook at home, and for about two weeks, you do just that. Every day, you'll eat some combination of eggs, cheese, red sauce, and pasta. *Every day.*

Mark my words: One night, swearing that you'll never touch a bowl of ramen again, you'll order pizza. And it will be all downhill from there.

Keep this in mind: Most of the world doesn't get to choose what they eat every day. You do. Most of the world would be appalled at how much food a typical American home wastes. You can decide yours won't be one of those homes. M. F. K. Fisher once said, "There is a communion of more than our bodies when bread is broken and wine is drunk"—and she's right. Food occupies the odd place of being both a necessity and a pleasure. Eating isn't like brushing your teeth, after all. Learning how to balance luxury and necessity in your meals is the key to truly enjoying and being thankful for what you eat.

Take heart, young chef. It takes several years and lots of experimentation to know how to shop and eat well. Until then, you'll throw away several pounds of questionable chicken, deliquescing lettuce, brown bananas, and clotted milk.

You Say To-MAY-to, I Say To-MAH-to

Before you head down the path of gustatory grownuphood, you'll need to figure out what kind of cook and eater you are. Maybe you *are* the type who can nosh on the same things day after day and never get sick of them. Or maybe you're a secret food snob, a Julia Child in waiting, who, alas, is stuck in a no-taste town. Maybe you *hate hate hate* cooking, and only did it because it was a chance to hang out with your favorite Uncle Frank.

Hot Cocoa

Makes enough mix to last you through the winter:

    4 cups instant nonfat dry milk

    5 tablespoons unsweetened cocoa

    $1\frac{1}{2}$ cups sugar

    $\frac{1}{8}$ tsp of salt

Optional for richer taste: half of the smallest jar of nondairy creamer and/or marshmallows if you like 'em

Shake in an airtight container to mix. Add $\frac{1}{3}$ cup of mix to a mug of hot water.

Instead of forcing yourself into a certain predetermined food regimen, have a test month to see what your eating/spending habits are like. Do you actually *like* grocery shopping, or do you dread that hour with a cart all week long? Does opening a menu make you dizzy with pleasure, or do you mostly eat out for the socializing? If you're like most, you prefer a bit of variety. It's your eating patterns that get stuck in a rut. Observe when you like to eat out and when you like to stay in. Does stress keep you out of the kitchen? Do you order in when you're depressed?

In terms of cooking at home, pay attention to what you throw out at the end of the week. Remember that a ton of groceries bought for one is not always the most cost-effective way of keeping yourself fed. Nor is buying a week's worth of groceries when you eat out almost every night. Despite your good intentions, you're wasting both money and food, making yourself feel guilty in the process.

You should try to develop a profile of your eating habits so that you can make your tummy happy while at the same time minimizing waste and expense. It may take a while, but you'll get the hang of it.

Going Out, Staying Cheap

Eating out is a pleasure that almost everyone enjoys. It's the way we socialize, the way we celebrate—it's even the way we cheer ourselves up. Unfortunately, it's also where we can drop the most cash—without even knowing it.

Let's take your average twentysomething urban office worker. We'll call her Nina. For breakfast, Nina stops by the coffee shop in her office building and drops $6 on a latte and a scone. Lunch she eats at her desk—$10 for a sandwich, a bottle of water, and some chips. Normally Nina would meet friends for dinner and drinks at a neighborhood café (upwards of $20), but tonight our urban go-go girl is feeling a tad broke, so she orders in for Chinese food because her refrigerator's empty and she's too tired to shop. There goes another tenner, plus $2 for tip.

How much has lovely Nina spent today? She'd rather not think about it, but *we* certainly can: around $28, and that doesn't include snacks. We'll make it an even $30. At a wage of $15 an hour as an editorial assistant, that's almost a third of Nina's daily income. And breaking it down is even scarier: $120 a month on coffee and scones alone, about $200 a month on sandwiches she eats at her desk.

Obviously something's got to change, but what? Nina doesn't like to cook, and while she might be convinced to, say, pack a sandwich in the morning, there's no way she's giving up her coffee, and eating dinner with friends is about more than just food. It's her emotional sustenance as well, and in her opinion, well worth a little extra money.

A lot of us are like Nina in that way. But that's no reason to end up in the poorhouse. There are lots of ways to eat out and still save money. And we don't mean McDonald's 24-7. Here are some of them.

Bargain Hunt

This doesn't just work at the mall. Restaurants often have coupons (two-for-one, or $10 discounts, for example) in the newspaper and on menu flyers. Another cheap way to eat out is to look for restaurants that offer specials—lunch and dinner buffets, pre–dinner rush discounts (usually during the "dead time" between four and seven in the evening), and prix fixe meals all fall under this category. And don't forget about happy-hour "pupus"—bar appetizers that can range from the exquisite (chicken satay, puff pastries, oysters) to the merely edible (popcorn and Vienna sausages).

Finally, we come to the greatest of all bargain inventions: the doggie bag. Only Europeans are snobbish about this wonderful Americanism. Just remember not to leave it at the table.

Phô, Anyone?

Despite what you might think, the best cheap food does not have to feature a variation on the hamburger/fried chicken/pizza theme. Depending on where you live, ethnic restaurants can offer the cheapest and healthiest food for a fraction of what you'd spend on a plate of overpriced pasta. So the décor might be a little funky and the foreign-language menus slightly daunting. Don't be afraid to ask the waiter or cook about the house specials. For the price of a meal, you'll also get an education and, if you're lucky, some new friends. Next time you come back, they'll probably have your table ready for you.

To help you on your culinary adventures, we'll offer a greatest-hits guide to ethnic cuisine.

- **Chinese:** Most folks who eat Chinese never venture beyond kung pao chicken and fried rice. While these are certainly good standbys (buffets offer these "standards" for $3 or $4 a plate), Chinese seafood is the real bargain, offering the freshest fish and shellfish at much less than they'd be at a Western-style restaurant. On the weekends, try a dim sum brunch (appetizer-style meals handed out from carts) as an alternative to bacon and eggs.

- **Caribbean:** Food from the islands can range from hot and spicy (Jamaican jerk chicken) to sweet and mild (Cuban fried plantains). But whether it's black beans and yellow rice or shrimp patties you crave, Caribbean cuisine offers staple food with lots of flavor and nutrition. The best bargains? Dominican/Puerto Rican/Cuban roast chicken for $4 a bird, and café con leche (latte without the designer price) at a buck.

- **Indian:** In New York's East Village, Indian food has filled the belly of many a starving artist. Indian entrees usually run about $8 a plate, and offer enough food for a few meals. Curries hold up well in the fridge, as does chicken biryani, a spicy dish with rice and raisins. Vegetarians will also appreciate the wide range of meat- and dairy-free dishes from which to choose.

- **Japanese:** Think Japanese is only for L.A. power lunches? Think again. Bento (Japanese "lunch boxes" complete with meat, vegetables, and rice) will run you about $7, while noodle shops ladle out huge portions of ramen and soba (wheat noodles) for about $5. In New York, check out the city's mysterious half-priced sushi restaurants. And miso soup and rice for $5 is still the best cure for a hangover that we know.

- **Mexican:** Hipsters in San Francisco's Mission District swear they have the best giant burritos in the world (about $5). Even if you're not on the West Coast, chances are there's a Mexican restaurant or taco truck somewhere nearby. Try carne asada (broiled steak) tacos with lots of lime juice and salsa. If you're really lucky, your neighborhood gets visited by the helado (ice cream) and mango (with lime and chile, eaten on a stick like a popsicle) vendors.

- **Middle Eastern:** Falafel (fried chickpea dumplings served in a pita) is both delicious and healthy, and will probably run you about $3. For variety, try chicken or lamb gyros. Just a little bit more, and just as yummy.

- **Southeast Asian:** Nowadays there's a Thai restaurant on every corner, and most cities have a few Vietnamese, Indonesian, and Malaysian restaurants as well. The scrumptious combination of fresh Asian ingredients—rice, noodles, vegetables, seafood, and meat—and delicate Indian spices has made Southeast Asian cuisine the new choice for takeout, as it's often cheaper and fresher than Chinese. Try phô, Vietnamese noodle soup, with its hearty blend of meat and vegetables for about $5 a bowl.

- **And More!** Of course there's more: Ethiopian for vegetarian food and lamb; Filipino for lumpia and chicken adobo; Korean for bi-bim-bab (rice in a hot pot with meat and veggies); and Greek for spanikopita (spinach pie). There's Eastern European delis, Swedish bakeshops, Hawaiian plate-lunch trucks, and Belgian *moules frîtes* (mussels and french fries) stands. Take a look around you; who lives where you live? Chances are there will be delicious, cheap restaurants of a similar stripe.

And the best part? After a while, eating McDonald's will seem exotic. You'll become more familiar with a range of ingredients and spices, perhaps even trying out a few recipes in your own kitchen. Cooking may even become, well, *creative*. Go figure.

Fear and Loathing in Aisle 7

So you're ready to do a little experimenting in the *cucina*, huh? But the idea of a grocery store scares you—all those fluorescent lights, endless aisles, coupons, wayward tots, tempermental carts, depressed house-husbands, "Lunchables"! Not to mention the sheer volume of *choice*. Thirty kinds of frozen juice is a few too many!

Not to worry, neophyte. We'll tackle shopping the same way the professionals do—with a list.

Seven Tips for Supermarket Bliss

1) Shop like Europeans do, a few items at a time, only buying the ingredients you'll need for that night's dish. If you're living in a city, this is more practical, and if you're cooking for one, you waste less. Plus, you get to carry one of those cute baskets and look like Audrey Hepburn or Marcello Mastrioanni. *Très* chic.

2) Twenty dollars for cereal, cheese, and some ice cream? Yup. As you probably know, brand, gourmet, and processed foods have the highest price tags. Cut your costs by buying generic

or store brands for basics like butter and milk. Make your own granola (toast oatmeal, dried fruit, nuts, and a little brown sugar in a shallow pan on low heat for about twenty minutes). But don't be a Scrooge. Allow yourself a few cherished items—cooking should be a treat, not a chore.

3) Unless it's a great deal, coupon clipping isn't worth your time. Do sign up for a discount card at your grocery store, however. It'll give you in-store discounts and (usually) check-cashing privileges.

4) As with ethnic restaurants, for the price of public transportation and a little walking, you can treat yourself to some truly exotic ingredients at ethnic grocery stores for much less than they'd go for in a gourmet shop.

5) Whether you're in the country or in the city, buying produce from local farmers' markets and vegetable stands ensures you the freshest ingredients (often organic) at the best prices. You're also directly supporting farmers, which in turn helps to protect rural land from succumbing to urban sprawl.

6) Join a co-op, especially if you're vegetarian or like to buy organic. If there's no co-op in your area, form a bulk-ordering club. Same food, cheaper than retail. You'll have to do some organizing (arrange for the food to be dropped off at a central location), but the money you save on premium organic food is well worth the time. (Again, go to www.cooperative.org for more information, or send a SASE to Co-op Directory Services, 919 21st Avenue South, Minneapolis, MN 55404 for a co-op or food buying club in your area.) Another option is Urban Organic, an organic produce wholesaler that delivers farm-fresh produce right to your door every week, nationwide (www.urbanorganic.com).

7) Through community-supported agriculture (CSA), you can sign up for subscription produce. Basically, you'll get a box of produce delivered to your house, or a central location, every week of the growing season (June through October). You'll get the usual—lettuce, tomatoes, corn—as well as veggies you've never heard of, like kohlrabi and jicama. CSAs also usually have work weekends and summer potlucks when you can visit the farm and play around in the dirt—a great way to reconnect with where your food comes from! (Find a CSA in your area through the U.S. Department of Agriculture's website: www.nal.usda.gov/afsic/csa/csastate.htm.)

Julia Who?

If the first items you purchased for your new home include a crêpe pan, a food processor, and an industrial-strength mixer, you can probably skip this section. If you think a food processor is someone who works at Burger King, we suggest you invest in a cookbook or two—they'll teach you much more about cooking than anything offered here.

Start with a basic technique-oriented cookbook like *Joy of Cooking*, Julia Child's *The Way to Cook*, or *The Silver Palate Cookbook* by Julee Rosso. Then you can branch out to your favorite types of cuisine. If you're vegetarian or vegan, Mollie Katzen's *Moosewood* series has delicious, healthy food, as does Deborah Madison's *The Savory Way*.

Learning how to be a good, creative cook takes years—don't sweat it if you make a few mistakes now and then. (Sometimes mistakes can be delicious. Write down where you went wrong and consider it your first original recipe!) There are, however, a few things to keep in mind as you experiment.

Rice, Beans, and Pasta

If you aren't already familiar with these lifesavers, you soon will be. They're grouped under the rather unappealing heading of "staples," and they'll provide the bulk of most of your meals. Beans are a terrific protein supplement for vegetarians, and don't forget how cheap pasta can be—a buck or less per box. Add to the holy trinity tuna fish, pancake/biscuit mix, and soup. Keep 'em in your pantry and replenish as needed.

Scary (and Not So Scary) Spice

Five hundred years ago, spices made the world go round. It's why Columbus bumped into the New World. He was looking for a shorter way to India and the East, the source of the yummy spices we're now familiar with, like pepper and cinnamon.

It's spice that makes our mouths water, so developing a good selection of herbs, oils, seasonings, and sauces will go a long way toward improving your cooking skills. Here's the short list. Consult your favorite cookbooks for more.

The Old Staple: Mac and Cheese (Version I)

$\frac{3}{4}$ cup macaroni

2 quarts boiling water

3 tablespoons butter

3 tablespoons flour

1 cup milk

$\frac{1}{4}$ teaspoon salt

$\frac{3}{4}$ cup grated cheddar cheese

Add macaroni to water. Melt butter, add flour mixed with seasonings, and stir until well blended. Pour milk in gradually while stirring constantly. Bring to boiling point. Boil two minutes. Add cheese gradually until melted.

(Source: *The Boston Cooking School Cook Book* by Fanny Merit Farmer, 1930 edition. Little, Brown and Company.)

> ### The Old Staple: Mac and Cheese (Version II)
>
> $\frac{1}{2}$ pound macaroni
>
> 8–10 tablespoons butter
>
> 1–1 $\frac{1}{2}$ cups shredded sharp cheddar cheese
>
> Salt and freshly ground pepper
>
> Cook the macaroni in boiling salted water until it is just tender. Be careful not to overcook it, lest it become very mushy. Drain. Butter a 2-quart baking dish, and arrange in it alternating layers of macaroni dotted with butter and shredded cheese. Season with salt and pepper, and top with a layer of cheese. Bake at 350 degrees until the cheese is melted and the macaroni is heated through.
>
> (Source: *James Beard's American Cookery*. Little, Brown and Company, 1972.)

The Essentials

The following is a list of spices that should be a part of every household—own them, learn them, love them: salt, pepper, hot sauce, garlic, balsamic vinegar, white wine, pepper, mustard, mayonnaise, soy sauce, olive oil, vegetable oil, chicken or veggie bouillon (for soup stock), brown and white sugar, and honey.

Herbs and Other Seasonings

You should also know rosemary, thyme, sage, basil (fresh if you can get it, or grow your own on a sunny windowsill or back porch), parsley, oregano, paprika, red pepper, cumin, curry paste or powder, cinnamon, nutmeg, and vanilla. Also try some of the pre-packaged Spanish rice seasonings (adobo and cilantro) for easy rice-and-bean meals with lots of flavor.

Guess Who's Coming to Dinner

The best way to get psyched about cooking? Entertain. Of course, hosting a big dinner party for all your friends is also a great way to stress yourself out, so plan accordingly. Looking for a fancy meal for about $20? Buy a bag of farm-raised mussels (about $4); steam them in white wine, garlic, and olive oil; and serve over a bed of linguini. French bread, some salad, a bottle of red wine, and that *chérie* you invited from work won't be able to resist.

Remember, too, that enjoying a bottle of good wine at home brings the price down to $2 or $3 a glass instead of the $5 or $6 you get charged in a restaurant. Check out wine listings online or in one of the wine magazines, and invest in a couple of good bottles at less than $15.

Potlucks are always fun (and cheap), as are informal coffee and bagel brunches. If you're ambitious and live in the same neighborhood as a few friends, a progressive dinner at a bunch of people's houses can be a great way to strengthen your sense of community (and raid your friends' alcohol stashes).

Go on picnics. Food *al fresco* is always more delicious. Especially in the summer, there's no reason to sit at home with the same old stuff. Grab a couple of different kinds of cheeses, some smoked sausage, French bread, an apple, and a bottle of wine and you've got a tasty meal.

Feed Me!

Finally, if you refuse to cook and you can't afford to eat out any longer, you can always rely on the kindness of strangers. Office parties and corporate functions almost always offer something to nibble on, as do gallery openings and literary readings. Of course, you'll have to hang around at least for a while and enjoy the scenery.

One perk of being a busboy/waiter is that you get fed. Don't underestimate how much money this can save you. Take advantage of any opportunities for free food. And if worse comes to worse, subsist on pizza until your parents to come into town. Then you can really splurge!

CHAPTER 5

The Practical Details of Living on Your Own

Now that you've got a roof over your head and some food in the fridge, you can finally experience what it's like to be truly independent. That's right—no parents, no teachers, no bedtime, no homework . . . and if you want, you can wait until April *15* to do your taxes! Heck, you can *choose your own health insurance!* Bank *wherever you like!* Pay your Visa minimum *or the whole darn thing!*

You get the point. Sure, being on your own is all about freedom—you can rock and roll all night and party every day. Or eat Pop Tarts and Cheez Whiz for dinner. But freedom is also all about taking care of business, managing the mundane, and dealing with the day-to-day. In other words, being, um, *responsible*— a concept first explained to you around second grade after a traumatic incident involving a pet fish and a toilet bowl.

Except that now, being responsible means more than just sprinkling food flakes into a tank once a day. It has to do with developing a healthy and self-respecting relationship with the world around you; determining where you fit in society; and understanding, and using to your advantage, the financial, political, and social forces at work in your destiny. It's about being—as Ben Franklin put it—healthy, wealthy, and wise.

And, of course, trying not to bounce *too* many checks along the way.

Personal Finance

We were getting along so well, then we had to go and bring up money. *Eew.* Can't we just go back to the food chapter? That was *much* more enjoyable.

Fortunately, there are many books that delve into personal finance far more deeply than this chapter will—for example, *Dollars and Sense for College Students* by Ellen Braitman (The Princeton Review/Random House, 1998) and *Your Money or Your Life: Transforming Your Relationship With Money and Achieving Financial Independence* by Joe Dominguez and Vicki Robin (Penguin, 1999). Consult one or both for more detailed information.

In the meantime, however, you'll need to master at least a few financial basics before we move on to chapter 6, where you'll be sorely tempted to blow all of those newly earned Benjamins. What's a how-to book without that old standby, the budget?

The Budget

Ah, the budget. That earnest series of columns and dollar-and-cent signs that offers the hopeful fantasy that you *really will* spend only $20 a month on "Miscellaneous" instead of the bewildering $156.73 that you actually end up shelling out.

Open any financial how-to book and you'll find a budget worksheet—complete with pre-selected categories like "Kids' Clothing" and "Lawn Care Supplies"— that may or may not reflect the realities of your individual life.

It's Your Money

- *Personal Finance for Dummies* by Eric Tyson, Mark Butler (editor), 3rd edition. IDG Books Worldwide, 2000.

- *The Complete Idiot's Guide to Personal Finance in Your 20s and 30s* by Sarah Young Fisher and Susan Shelly. Macmillan, 1999.

- *The Wall Street Journal Guide to Understanding Money & Investing* by Kenneth M. Morris, Virginia B. Morris, and Alan M. Siege. Fireside, 1999.

- *1,001 Perfectly Legal Ways to Get Exactly What You Want, When You Want It, Every Time* by FC&A.

- *Your Money or Your Life: Transforming Your Relationship With Money and Achieving Financial Independence* by Joe Dominguez and Vicki Robin. Penguin, 1999.

- *1,001 Ways to Save, Grow, and Invest Your Money* by David E. Rye. Career Press, 1999.

The bottom line: Is a budget worth your time? Depends on what kind of person you are financially. Some folks really dig the "down to the penny" thing and do it every month. They are probably the people who *least* need a budget, since they've already worked out what they spend on what and keep themselves in check naturally. Others get so wrapped up in fancy financial software and graphing capabilities and allocating and tracking every 43 cents that they forget the original purpose of the budget: to (a) live within your means and (b) make your money work for you. That means acknowledging what kind of lifestyle works best with your goals and personality and managing your money accordingly.

Say you're a med student receiving loans that will leave you with $80,000 of debt after graduation. You've made a conscious choice, based on future earnings potential, to spend more than you earn right now. On the other hand, say you're pulling down $60,000 a year right out of college as a software designer, and you're at the office so much you don't have time to spend the money you're making. Now would be the right time to save and invest as much as possible. That way you'll have a little bit of a cushion in case career plans change a few years down the road.

Whatever your particular financial circumstances, one thing holds true: if you spend more than you earn, you go into debt. *Period.* While significant debt ($50,000 and up) in student loans and on credit cards is a reality for many people in their twenties and thirties, just because it's on paper doesn't mean it's not real money. And with interest rates in the 20 percent range on some credit cards, you can be certain that you'll be paying off those bills for *decades* to come.

So, keeping track of expenses and income for at least one month is certainly worth it. Get a little notebook and make note of what you *actually* spend—not what you *think* you should spend. That includes the big stuff, like rent and utilities, as well as every little cup of coffee, every newspaper, every buck left at a bar as a tip. Keep tabs on what you take in, too, and don't leave out under-the-table gigs and the random twenties that Mom slips you when she comes to visit on the weekend.

For the most part, you should be somewhere in the range of the following spending plan:

Housing:	20–35%
Food:	15–30%
Personal debt:	10–20%
Transportation:	6–20%
Utilities:	4–7%
Clothing:	3–10%
Personal care:	2–4%
Insurance:	4–6%
Health:	2–8%
Miscellaneous items:	1–4%
Savings:	5–9%

(Source: Consumer Credit Counseling Service of the Gulf Coast Area)

From the information you've gathered, set up a system for yourself of what you can spend where. If you find that it works for you, continue. If not, scrap it and try again. Remember that a budget it not about deprivation; sometimes too much penny-pinching can backfire, causing you to overspend because you feel like you've "earned it." More than anything, your budget should be moderate and flexible, allowing for treats now and then, scaling back when and where you need it.

It's in the Bank (You Hope)

With account fees ranging as high as $40 a month in some areas, shopping around for the best banking deal is well worth your time and energy. Most likely, you already have an account from your college days or from your hometown. Before you close that account and open a new one, make sure that you're getting a better deal. So much banking is done by phone, computer, and mail right now that it might not be necessary to have a branch right next to you.

For example, say that in your hometown savings bank, you've got free checking, no minimum balance, and a line of credit should you need to take out an emergency loan. Your parents bank there, too, and you know a few of the tellers by name. They even covered you the last time you bounced a check—without charging a fee. The only downside to keeping your account there is the $2 they charge for each out-of-network ATM withdrawal (plus the buck or so most nonproprietary ATMs now charge for a transaction). At five or six withdrawals per month, that's about $15. If that's less or comparable to what you'd pay in fees at your new bank, consider staying where you are, especially if you've got a good working relationship. In this world of mega-mergers—where the most connection you have with your money is a recorded voicemail or mouse click—being able to talk to a live human being about your money is worth an extra few bucks.

If you do decide to shop around for a new account, there are a few things to keep in mind.

- The type of bank you choose will dictate the kind of service you can expect to get. Commercial banks (Citibank, Bank of America, Key Bank, etc.) are bigger and are less customer-friendly (unless you open a big corporate account). Savings banks offer checking and savings accounts, auto loans, and mortgages. Credit unions—nonprofit financial institutions—are usually more consumer-friendly, offering better rates on loans and fewer requirements for no-fee checking. Keep in mind that many employers offer special no-fee relationships with certain banks, as well as the usual services like direct deposit of your paycheck. Check with your human resources officer for more information.

- Most banks offer a basic or "no-frills" account, geared toward low-income, low-transaction customers. Check the fine print on these—many have limits on the number of checks you can write and ATM withdrawals you can make. What's the fee if you go over your limit? Is there a minimum balance? Are there extra charges if you conduct your business using a real live teller rather than an ATM? Also, how much will you be charged to make withdrawals from non-network ATMs? (Remember that the fee stays constant no matter how much or little you take out. Minimize your fees by withdrawing enough money to last you a while.) Will your bank help you with other services, such as personal loans or credit cards?

- Check to see if your bank offers a debit card, which looks and behaves like a credit card, except you don't have the benefit of a grace period. A debit card may be a good option if you're trying to curb your debt, as the cost of purchases is deducted immediately out of your account. (Make sure to ask whether there are any monthly fees for this service.)

- Finally, what are the overdraft (bounced check) fees for your account, and how much will they cover you for? Remember that bounced checks can cost you as much as $50 in fees (from both the merchant and the bank). Avoid them by balancing your account every month.

To open an account, you'll need your Social Security number, money to deposit (cash, check, or money order), an ID (driver's license or passport), and your signature (but we'll assume you carry that with you).

Carded

You probably don't need much convincing, but if you don't have a credit card already, now is the time to get one. Whether you actually use it or not, a credit card is often required to reserve any number of consumer items—from airline tickets, rental cars, and hotel rooms to video store cards and concert tickets.

There are other reasons to use plastic as well. First of all, it builds up your credit record, which you'll need for future loans. Also, most credit card companies offer extended guarantees for purchases made on the card. At the very least, any merchandise that was more than $50 and was purchased with your credit card within 100 miles of your home address should be covered under the card's "charge-back protection" agreement. That means if you have a disagreement with a merchant about goods or services rendered, you can have the charge erased from your account. Finally, a credit card can really be a lifesaver in case of an emergency. That gives you plenty of reasons to get set up with a no-fee, low-interest card *that you pay off every month.*

In other words, a credit card is *not* a reason to go into debt or buy things you can't afford. Don't be fooled: credit is debt, no matter which way you slice it, and you'll be charged interest for the privilege of carrying it. Interest rates usually range from about 10 percent (at the low end) to as much as 24 percent (at the bloodsucking end). Choosing your credit card wisely—just as you did your bank—could mean saving hundreds of dollars on interest payments and fees. If you're in the market for a new card, or switching from an old one, consider the following:

- **Interest and fees:** This includes the APR (annual percentage rate) of interest, any yearly (or monthly) service fees, and late payment charges. Unless you're planning on charging big-ticket items ($10,000 or more), mileage and other affinity cards are probably not worth the annual fees (usually in the $50 range) and high interest rates (upwards of 20 percent). Similarly, look carefully at the fine print on cards that offer ridiculously low teaser rates (often about 5 percent for your first three months, but jumping to 24 percent thereafter). Your best bet is to shop around for a low monthly rate—contact www.cardtrak.com for a list of low-rate credit cards, or check your state's banking homepage (New York's, for example, is www.state.banking.ny.us) for more information. Note that cards like American Express and Diners Club are charge cards, not credit cards. You'll be required to pay the entire bill off every month or else face steep penalties.

- **Grace period:** The grace period is the number of days after your purchase that you must pay your bill. You'll want a credit card that offers a standard grace period (about four weeks). Use this perk—essentially an interest-free loan—to your advantage by paying your entire bill off every month.

- **Credit limit:** Don't be swayed into signing up for a card with an outrageously high credit limit. If it's way beyond your means, it will only tempt you to spend more, and you'll end up paying for it through high interest rates or hidden monthly fees.

Finally, a few last words of credit advice:

- Remember that the more cards you have, the more you'll owe. For most folks, two pieces of plastic is plenty.

- If you can't pay off the whole thing each month, at least try to pay more than the minimum.

- If you're barely making your minimum, using your card to cover food and rent, paying your bills with cash advances, or you don't need an alarm clock because debt collectors wake you up in the morning—well, it's time to cut up your cards. You've got a debt problem. Which brings us to . . .

Seeing Red

Most of us carry some kind of debt, which ranges from a simple electric bill to something as complicated as a mortgage on a house. Usually, bill paying is as easy as writing a check and putting it in the mail (and can be even easier now, with automatic electronic deductions and Web bill-payment services). However, if you're up to your ears in student loans and credit card bills, you may need a little help sorting out what you owe and to whom.

Student Loans

Depending on your work/student status, you may be able to qualify for a deferment or partial cancellation of your student loans. Contact your university's student loan officer for more information. You don't want to default, which will send your credit record into a tailspin.

Debt Consolidation

While this won't erase what you owe, it will make it easier to track your payments and, perhaps, inch your interest rate down a bit. Again, ask your lender about debt consolidation options, or contact Debt Counselors of America at www.dca.org.

Don't Be Afraid to Ask for Help

The National Foundation for Consumer Credit is a nonprofit organization that offers credit counseling services nationwide. Call 800-338-2227 (or check on the Web at www.nfcc.org) to locate a debt counselor near you. They'll help you set up a budget and, if necessary, work directly with lenders to lower your interest rates and set up a payment plan to get you back on track.

Seeing Red: The Warning Signs
• You think of credit as cash, not debt.
• Your debts are greater than your assets.
• You owe more than seven creditors.
• You are an impulsive or compulsive shopper.
• You don't know how much your monthly living expenses are or the amount of your total debt.
• Your expected increase in income is already committed to paying off debts.
• You have to pay back several installment payments that will take more than twelve months to pay off.
• You get behind in utility or rent payments.
• You have to consolidate several loans into one or reduce monthly payments by extending current loans in order to pay your debts.
• You cannot afford to pay for regular living expenses or credit payments; therefore, you take out a loan, withdraw savings, skip payments, or pay only the minimum amount due on your charge accounts.

Back in Black

The opposite of debt is savings, which is exactly what you'll have if you start stashing away the dough *now*. Whether it's a regular old interest-bearing savings account, a certificate of deposit (CD) or money market account through your local bank, or an individual retirement fund (IRA), squirreling a little bit each month will have *mucho* benefits later in life, when your earning potential decreases with age. Much has been made in recent years of how much money you'd end up with in a retirement fund if you'd started saving when you were 25 instead of 35. Take heed! Since interest paid on IRAs accrues with each passing year, the earlier you start, the better. Plus, the money you put in isn't taxed until you withdraw it, an added incentive. Finally, certain types of educational IRAs allow for penalty-free early withdrawals to pay for educational expenses, something to keep in mind if you're planning on graduate school someday.

These days, it seems like everyone (and their pimply teenaged brother) is playing the stock market. Before you set your afternoons aside for a little day trading, however, make sure that you (a) educate yourself about the market and any investments you might be making and (b) have a strong stomach for risk. Also, weigh any possible gain against what you're paying out as interest on loans. If you're making 10 percent on an investment but paying 18 percent on your credit card bill, your money may be better spent paying off your debt.

Hey, Hey, I'm the Taxman

Your early twenties may be the only time in your life when you actually look forward to tax time. If you're not making much, you could qualify for a refund—or at least break even. So take advantage of your meager wages and file early. You can also deduct student loan interest payments, as well as qualified educational expenses—including post-graduate and continuing education—through the Hope scholarship tax credit. If your income is truly limited (about $10,000 or less per single adult) or if you have dependents, you could also qualify for an earned income credit (EIC), which will add another $1,000 or so to your refund. Checks take approximately six weeks to arrive, or you can opt to have your refund automatically sent to your bank account via direct deposit.

Or, you may be like most Americans, moaning and groaning all the way until April 15. Either way, don't believe what your tax-evading friends tell you; if you made money, the IRS will find out about it, no matter how insignificant the amount. And when the IRS does catch up with you, what might have been just a few hundred bucks will have grown significantly. (They charge interest and late fees, you know, just like the credit card companies.) All reasons to grin and bear it. File an extension if you need to—late payments begin to accrue penalties and interest as soon as the clock strikes midnight on April 16. (Fortunately, no pumpkins are involved.)

There are about a zillion ways to file your taxes these days, from retail software programs like Intuit's TurboTax and Kiplinger's TaxCut to hiring a tax professional (a very good idea if you're an artist or self-employed—ask around for a recommendation or hoof it on over to H&R Block, www.hrblock.com). If you're the do-it-yourself type, simply click over to the mother of all tax websites, the beloved www.irs.ustreas.gov, where groovy graphics and lots of exclamation points lamely try to convince you that doing your taxes is fun!

A few things to keep in mind as you near that cruelest of all months:

- If you're single and you claim zero exemptions on your W-4 (that inexplicably long form you fill out for each job where you just write "1" or "0" and then sign your name), you'll get more back at the end. If you claim one exemption, you'll probably either owe a little or break even.

- Just because your W-2s couldn't find you doesn't mean the IRS won't be able to. Keep track of where you worked and how much you earned on each job. If you don't receive a W-2 by mid-March, contact your employer and ask for another copy at your new address.

- If you're self-employed or an independent contractor (e.g., freelance writer, graphic designer, housepainter), you might be required to file your taxes quarterly. You could also be deducting certain expenses (like a home office, professional training, or travel). Contact a tax professional for more help on this one—and do not throw away any of your 1099 forms. Those record untaxed independent contractor income, money you can be sure the IRS knows about.

- Unless you're the lucky resident of a state like Oregon or New Hampshire (*Live Free or Die!*), where there are no state taxes, on April 15 you'll also be required to file state, and possibly local, taxes. Residents of the Big Apple are blessed with the trifecta of paying taxes to the IRS, to the state of New York, *and* to New York City.

- State and local taxes become *particularly* engrossing if you've moved a few times in a year. There's a tax form for every kind of resident: part-time, part-year, nonresidents, former residents, etc. You get the picture. If you made money there, you owe something.

Who's Got You Covered?

It's your Uncle Len's favorite topic of conversation; it takes up *far* too much ad space on television; it's the source of half of the junk mail you receive; and to you, it appears to be a strange and mysterious subculture. It's called insurance, and it goes something like this (with gusto!): *whole-life, term-life, actuary, annuity. Premium, deductible, agent, disability.* In case of insomnia, repeat over and over again until you fall asleep.

Insurance is, unfortunately, one of those "facts of life," though not as interesting as the ones you learned about in fourth grade. Most likely you've had medical insurance for years *without even knowing it!* Mom and Dad filled out the forms; you just showed up for the appointments.

As frightening as it may seem, there's a whole world of insurance out there besides your basic health coverage, and now that you're an adult (gulp!), it's time to familiarize yourself with some of the biggies. You should look into (in order of necessity) health, renter's, disability and life, and auto insurance.

Health Insurance

Employed or no, being covered is an absolute *requirement* in this day and age. If you're a full-time worker, most likely your employer is required by law to provide you with a health insurance plan—probably an HMO (health maintenance organization) or PPO (preferred provider organization), whereby you see plan-approved doctors for a co-payment of about $10, more if they are "out of network." HMOs love acronyms, so don't get sidetracked by all the capital letters: PCP stands for your primary care physician (who coordinates your treatments and must approve any visits to specialists), while WHC can be short for women's health coordinator. If you're a woman, you can usually elect your WHC as your PCP, since this is the doctor whom you'll probably see most regularly. (And, while you're at it, don't forget to RSVP your CEO and CC it to the VP of M&As over at MSN ASAP. OK?)

If you do end up paying medical bills out of your pocket, make sure to keep your receipts for reimbursement. Include in your reimbursement letter your contact information, your Social Security number, your doctor's name, and any procedural codes listed on the receipt. Make a copy and then wait a few *months* for your money to arrive—insurance companies can be pretty slow when it comes to paying you back, so pester them every few weeks or so with a phone call.

If you're unemployed, self-employed, or otherwise not covered, there are several health insurance options for you. Some states, like Hawaii and Oregon, have universal coverage laws, guaranteeing insurance for all residents. Between jobs? Look into COBRA (Consolidated OmniBus Reconciliation Act), which requires that your former employer extend your health plan for up to 18 months after you leave. There are also several private companies that offer both short- and long-term individual coverage. Finally, there's the nonprofit Blue Cross/Blue Shield, which guarantees coverage for anyone who applies (www.bluecares.com). Remember that the higher your deductible, the lower the cost of your insurance; if you're just trying to avoid bankrupting yourself or your family, you might think about a deductible in the $500 to $1,000 range.

Full dental and vision insurance is rarer and rarer these days. If you've got a plan, consider yourself lucky. If not, there's probably a LensCrafters or Pearle Vision nearby, which can provide frames and a full exam for as little as $150. As for your pearly whites, keep them in good shape by brushing and flossing, look for a lower-cost dentist for routine work, and consider letting the almost-professionals at a nearby dental school take care of some of the more expensive work. You'll get high-quality treatment and the latest technology at a significantly lower price.

Renter's Insurance

Heard of homeowner's insurance? Renter's insurance is the same idea, but for those of us who like our shelter by the month. It's a simple concept: Shell out a couple hundred bucks a year (depending on the value of your belongings) to protect your stuff against fire, theft, or other disaster. Look in the Yellow Pages and shop around for the best rates. Don't forget to ask about a discount if you have a smoke detector or fire extinguisher.

Disability and Life Insurance

Disability insurance protects you in case of a debilitating accident or disease that renders you unable to work to support yourself. Most likely your employer will offer some form of disability insurance—whether it be temporary (TDI, temporary disability insurance), long-term, or worker's compensation (for accidents on the job). If you're self-employed but would still like to be protected against disability, contact a local insurance provider and ask about an individual policy. For young people without dependents, unless your employer offers life insurance, don't waste your money.

Automobile Insurance

The best thing about car insurance is that you need it only if you have a car. The worst thing is that if you *do* have a car, auto coverage is not only required by law, but its cost is dependent on your driving record, your gender, your age, where you live, and your car's make, model, and color. (Maybe you didn't *have* to buy that cherry-red Mustang, but who could resist?). Fortunately, in recent years national insurance companies like Geico (www.geico.com) have lowered rates in notoriously high-premium states like California. Check around for the best rates in both national and local insurers, and don't forget to get yourself an AAA membership (www.aaa.com), which is still the best deal around for emergency roadside assistance and travel planning.

The Home Office-ette

Unfortunately, all this "taking care of business" usually requires at least occasional access to a computer and printer, as well as the Internet, and it also generates *a lot* of paperwork. Whether you like it or not, you're going to have to figure out a way of getting to a computer and organizing your personal files. Consider setting up a mini–home office for yourself, keeping the following in mind:

- **Computer:** If you're already wired, great. If not, and you're thinking about buying a computer, realize that there are as many PC styles, prices, and vendors as there are people. The cost of a basic setup is falling every *day*, it seems, so don't feel pressured into buying a system that's beyond your budget. Remember, too, that some retailers sell refurbished older models with upgraded memory and a faster processing speed for as little as $800 for the whole setup. Rather be unplugged? Unless you're affiliated with a university, it can be tough to find low-cost, dependable computer rentals. Copy shops like Kinko's and some Internet cafés offer computer services by the hour, but they're expensive. If you're paying for a rental more than a few times a week, consider investing in a system you can call your own.

- **Printers:** Many PCs these days come bundled with an inkjet printer, which boasts graphic-quality printing at a low price (as little as $100). Sound too good to be true? As with many "deals," there's a catch: Refilling those pesky ink cartridges costs about $25 a pop, and you'll go through one every few months. After about a year, you'll have spent as much as you would have spent on a personal laser printer at $299 (its toner cartridges last about 5,000 pages).

- **Peripherals:** Personal digital assistants, or PDAs, like the Palm Pilot, are all the rage these days, as are CD burners and MP3 players. Follow your tastes here, though we'd recommend some kind of portable storage disk (like a Zip drive) for backing up or transporting large files that can't fit on a regular floppy.

- **Software:** If you're still affiliated with a university—or know anyone who is—you can get major discounts on all kinds of name-brand software. Microsoft Office has everything you need to create documents, keep track of expenses and scheduling, and access the Internet and e-mail. A good accounting program (with check-writing and account-balancing functions) is Quicken, available in both Windows and Macintosh versions.

Record-Keeping

Whether you keep track of receipts, tax returns, old bills, and account statements on the computer or the old fashioned way with file boxes (most of us do both), you'll have to find a way to store everything with minimal clutter and disorganization. Just putting everything in one big folder (digital or manila) isn't going to help you find anything. Spend some time cleaning out what you have, and then develop a system that you can stick with in the future. I usually do my bill-paying, record-keeping, and filing once a month, and then do a big cleanout every year. How long should you keep stuff? Hold on to tax returns for at least seven years, loan statements for the life of the loan, credit card and bank statements for a year, and other bills only until your payment has cleared. If you're itemizing your deductions, ask your accountant (or consult the appropriate IRS publication) for a list of what records you should be keeping.

One Day at a Time

There's *more*? Other than food, shelter, money, a couple of credit cards, three kinds of insurance, a professional filing system, an accountant, and maybe a personal assistant or two to keep track of all your paperwork, what else could you need?

Despite what this chapter may be leading you to think, day-to-day survival (even *thrive*-al) really is about more than personal finance, taxes, and filing. Here's a rundown of the best of the rest.

Transportation

The real question to ask yourself here is, "Do I really need a car?" If you're in an area with good public transportation, no matter how expensive you think those bus passes are, they're a helluva lot cheaper than paying for insurance and gas, not to mention parking, tolls, city permits, and maintenance. Trains and buses get even cheaper if your city offers an employee fare program, like New York City's TransitChek (where company workers can buy their passes with pre-tax dollars). On the other hand, don't sacrifice your safety for a few bucks. If it's late, you're alone, and you're without wheels, take a cab.

Clothing

Shopping is probably the one thing you *don't* need advice on. Okay, maybe just a little:

- One word: *Sale.*

- One more word: *Discount.*

- The great thing about revolving fashions is that you have to wait only a few decades or so for something to come back into style, which makes shopping at thrift and vintage stores even more fun.

- Shopping out of season saves your bank account, especially on expensive things like coats and (who would have thought so little could cost so much?) summer bikinis.

- A quality item of clothing that you'll have for years is usually worth a dozen el cheapos.

Active Citizenship

This includes practical responsibilities like voting and jury duty, as well as the more nebulous stuff like community involvement, volunteering, and simply being a good neighbor. If you move to a new place, make sure you register to vote. (Some states register you when you get a driver's license; otherwise call your local voter registration office, which should be listed in the front pages of the phone book.) If you get called for jury duty, *don't blow it off.* You can get charged hefty fines for not showing up, and many states are tightening up on their enforcement. Plus, the whole court thing is pretty interesting.

The point is to get to know the place where you're living. Who are your council members, state and federal representatives, senators? (Information about contacting federal elected officials can be found on the Internet through HPI PoliticalInfoSystem at www.hpi.com.) What kind of work are community organizations doing in your area? Are there ways you can get involved? If you're not the joiner type, look in the alternative weeklies or on bulletin boards for individual volunteer opportunities, like adult and child literacy training, park conservation, or after-school arts programs. When I lived in Chicago, I played Scrabble with a 95-year-old gentleman named Horace—nicknamed "Hockey." I've beaten many a competitor with the two- and three-letter words he taught me (aa, azo, qat). Not to mention what I learned about bluffing!

Health and Well Being

Last and most important, it's actually true: Prevention *is* the best medicine, though when you're young and healthy, long-term well being is probably the last thing on your mind—especially during your twenties, when you're most likely to experiment with a range of lifestyles and behaviors. Developing good habits now, though, is probably the best thing you can do for later. Besides the usual (eat well, drink lots of water, and exercise regularly), taking care of yourself means looking after your personal safety; monitoring your alcohol, tobacco, and drug use; practicing safe sex; getting enough sleep; and spending a little time just being quiet with yourself. Remember, too, that many places offer health and well-being services.

Hospitals and clinics have free HIV, HCV (Hepatitis C), and STD testing, as well as mental health and substance abuse counseling, programs to quit smoking, and support group services. Churches, synagogues, community centers, and even some employers offer counseling and educational programming as well. And don't forget the nationwide networks geared toward helping folks: Alcoholics Anonymous (AA), Narcotics Anonymous (NA), Adult Children of Alcoholics (ACOA), the Gay Men's Health Crisis (GMHC), the American Cancer Society, and many others too numerous to mention.

CHAPTER 6

Now *That's* Entertainment

Cheap entertainment? Easy, you say. You've got a TV, a VCR, and a connection to the Internet. And if there's nothing on—or you're bored with surfing—there's always the movies. Who cares if you don't get out much? You see Gwyneth once in a while, and of course Cameron, Tiger, Mary J., Drew, Ethan, and Johnny. You know, *the crew.*

Do you know more about Puff Daddy's social life than you do your own? That's called a warning sign. *You don't get out enough!* There are others:

- Your closest friends are named Joey, Chandler, Ross, Rachel, Phoebe, and Monica.

- You know how to Instant Message, and do so . . . all the time.

- You think "chatting" requires a keyboard.

- Your range of emotions is limited to :) and ;) and : (

- When you finally *do* get out, you find life sort of weird without that two-inch frame around it.

So maybe I'm exaggerating. But it's true—we spend way too much time in front of little black boxes (or big silver screens, if you're into movies). If you're going to thrive as well as survive, to learn about yourself and other people, you'll need to see a little of the world—not to mention your own backyard. It's time to get out of the house and onto the streets (or courts, or parks, or rooftops, or stages). Here's a whole calendar's worth of not-so-expensive stuff to do. Try one or all.

Finding It

First you've got to find the stuff. Consult newspapers, alternative weeklies, magazines, and the Web for listings. A few hints:

- **Be spontaneous!** Most media listings have both a "weekend" section that lists all the goings-on about town for the following week, as well as a onetime listing for the whole month. If you see something you like, write down all the information in your personal calendar, even if the event's a couple weeks away. That way, as you get close to the date, you can decide whether you're still up for it. If you're sure you want to check it out, make sure to buy or reserve your tickets in advance where applicable.

- **Sign up:** At most performance events, galleries, and bookstores, there's a mailing list. Put your name on it to be alerted to listings that don't always get put in the newspaper. That also goes for websites that you like, as well as major newspapers and magazines that have e-mail update services.

- **Membership has its privileges:** If you're a frequent attendee of a certain theater, gallery, or museum, consider becoming a member. You'll get discounts on admission, an events calendar, special invitations to parties, and private previews. (Check with your parents on this one—they might already have a family membership, which means that kids can get benefits, too.)

- **Everyone's a critic:** Why not you? Volunteer to be an entertainment or restaurant reviewer for a local rag or website. Even if they don't pay, you'll get your tickets and meals free, as well as some writing samples. Once you get a portfolio of your articles together (called "clips"), you can call yourself freelance and get paid!

- **Sold out:** If you can't get a ticket you want, don't give up hope. There are lots of sources for other tickets, from Ticketmaster alternatives (type "tickets" or "tickets online" into your search engine for current listings) to auction sites (www.ebay.com and others) and the classifieds. Or you can always show up at the venue and look for people with extra tickets.

Going Clubbing

Not just for the Scouts or high-class suburbanites anymore, there are now clubs for just about every interest or hobby, from Scrabble to soccer to spelunking. Check in the paper and at places like sports stores and the local co-op. Or hook into an Internet listserv or discussion group in your chosen field and ask around for groups that meet in your area. (For a comprehensive listing of Internet discussion groups, go to CataList, the official catalog of listserv lists, at www.lsoft.com/lists/listref.html.) Some groups you may be able to find nearby:

- **Parlez-vous Urdu?** Language clubs often meet at local ethnic restaurants, where tongues (and alcohol) may flow more freely.

- **Touchdown!** Meet people every week in the park for a pick-up game of soccer, Ultimate Frisbee, rugby, or softball. If you want something more formal, your company might have a sports team, or look for what's regionally popular: e.g., volleyball in California, bowling in Wisconsin, canoe paddling in Hawaii, lacrosse in Connecticut, polo in Palm Beach—chances are there will be a league you can join.

- **Alma mater forever:** Don't forget to join your college's alumni association for access to social, networking, and athletic events. Some alumni groups even maintain their own clubhouses (as most of the Ivies do in NYC), sponsoring events and giving old geezers in green pants a place to hang out and read the paper.

- **Calling all Village People:** The YMCA/YWCA offers a lower-cost alternative to your run-of-the mill overpriced health club. Plus, there's usually a pool and a sauna, and lots of nice older ladies around that inexplicably smile at you when you pass by them.

- **Tree-huggers unite:** Environmental organizations like the Sierra Club (www.sierraclub.org) and the Nature Conservancy (www.tnc.org) run outdoor activities all year long. Contact the chapter in your area for guided day hikes, work days (clearing brush and non-native species, for example), and other educational programming.

Helping Hands

Give a little and you'll get a lot back. Volunteering is a great way to meet people, form community ties, and get to know your neighborhood. Plus, you'll have experiences that will last you a lifetime.

- **Gimme shelter:** Domestic violence and homeless shelters need food servers, intake operators, shift counselors, literacy volunteers, and GED tutors.

- **These are the people in your neighborhood:** CityCares groups (www.citycares.org) all around the country organize volunteer projects in partnership with community-based agencies, then recruit and manage teams of volunteers to staff the project. Most of these projects take place before or after regular work hours or on the weekends.

- **Afterschool special:** With school funding cuts, there's always room for more help around the classroom. Be an academic tutor; arts, crafts, and music teacher; or athletic coach. Look into the Boys and Girls Club in your area for more information (www.bgca.org).

- **Play in the dirt:** Feel the urge to commune with nature? Volunteer through a local farm or Community Supported Agriculture (CSA) program; adopt a section of a nearby park, forest area, or botanical garden; or contact an environmental organization for more information about work days (see listings above).

- **Big Brother is watching:** Big Sister, too! Create a long-lasting relationship with a child—and reawaken the kid inside you, too—through Big Brothers Big Sisters of America (www.bbbsa.org).

- **Homeward bound:** Learn building skills while you help families in need. Contact a nonprofit home-building organization like Habitat for Humanity (www.habitat.org) for information about upcoming projects.

- **Pet rocks don't snuggle:** Your local Humane Society and SPCA (Society for the Prevention of Cruelty to Animals) need help caring for ownerless animals. If you're in the city and miss Fido, consider spending a few hours a week giving some attention to those who need it.

The Great Outdoors

Even for big-city dwellers, getting away from the hustle and bustle is easier than you thought. A few suggestions about how to make Mother Nature your friend:

- **Saturdays (or Tuesdays or Mondays) in the park:** Play some hoops, have a picnic, read a book, take a long walk, or just snooze under the trees during your lunch break. Lots of parks offer nighttime activities as well. From outdoor movies to summer music festivals (usually free, and if they're not, sit outside the gates—same sound, much lower price) and bandstand performances, it's always better under the stars.

- **Yodel-ay-hee-hoo!** Many places—even densely populated urban areas—have good hiking just a few hours away. Look into what you can access by train and bus, or contact your local outdoors/ camping store, Sierra Club, or Nature Conservancy for information about guided hikes and tours.

- **Head for the hills:** They can be a year-round destination. In summer there's hiking, and in winter there's skiing, snowboarding, and sledding. Mountaineering and ski clubs, singles groups, and alumni associations run weekend trips a few times a season.

- **Take a walk:** The best way to get to know a place is by walking its streets. Meander around your neighborhood on a sunny afternoon. Or, if you have time after work one night, walk the length of your favorite avenue, top to bottom . . . just to see what's there.

- **Get wet:** If you're lucky enough to live near a body of water (even a public pool can do the trick), see what's available. Probably more than you realize—from boat and ferry rides (San Francisco's Sausalito ferry is only $4.80 round-trip) and canoe and kayak rentals to swimming, surfing, and waterskiing.

- **Spinning your wheels:** Skateboarder? Rollerblader? Cyclist? Look for a nearby bike path and get rolling.

- **Don't know much about biology:** Depending on where you live, you may have a good botanical garden, zoo, or aquarium nearby. Impress people with your knowledge of hermaphroditic worms and flesh-eating plants. Great party banter!

You've Got Class

Most colleges and universities—private and public—offer continuing/adult education programs. Whether you're in it for graduate credits or just for fun, taking a class is a good way to transition out of undergrad. Not only are you getting out and meeting people, but you're learning something at the same time.

- **Texts and the city:** City and community colleges are the best place to look for cheap classes in arts and crafts, languages, and dance, as well as more practical things like computer programming, software, and Internet instruction.

- **Underwater basket weaving:** If you want to pay a little bit more, try a private school, academy, or organization that specializes in your unique interest: glassblowing, bartending, wine tasting, African dance, photography, life drawing . . . .

- **Online instruction:** If you'd rather do your learning remotely, Barnes & Noble has just started offering free online classes with fun choices like Introduction to Jazz as well as computer programming, financial planning, and health and wellness. It doesn't get you out of the house, but it's an interesting option. Go to www.bn.com.

- **Write it off:** Remember that some of your continuing education expenses may qualify you for a deduction under the government's Hope scholarship. Go to www.irs.ustreas.gov for more information.

Belles Lettres

You don't necessarily have to take a class to have a rich intellectual and literary life. Here are a few ways to keep yourself thinking—on the cheap.

- **Dot-org:** Educational, civic, and cultural organizations—even some corporations—offer a whole calendar's worth of readings, panel discussions, and lectures. (How else do you keep all those socialites busy?) Most are free or very cheap. Ask about student prices even if you've already graduated. If you look young, they might not ask to see an ID.

- **Author, author:** Libraries and bookstores are other places where you can go for readings, book signings, and discussions. See your favorite writer up close, ask questions, get inspired!

- **Book and writing groups:** Get a few people together to discuss someone else's writing or your own. Many bookstores offer discount rates to book club members and can even give help on getting one organized. *The New York Times* also offers book and writing discussion groups online. Go to www.nyt.com and look under "Forums." As for writing, take a look at *The Portable Creative Writing Workshop,* by Pat Boran (Salmon Poetry, 1999), for suggestions on how to run a workshop for yourself or with friends.

Galleries and Museums

So maybe you have bad memories of being dragged through room after room of Dead White Males and English countrysides as a child. In recent years, galleries and museums have made big efforts to reach out to their communities with new programming and better, more interactive exhibits. Now, it seems, there's a museum for every interest: contemporary sculpture, video and digital art, rock and roll, film and television, photography, ethnic studies, natural history, astronomy, science and industry—even schlock has its own repository. (The Museum of Bad Art in Boston has an impressive collection of clown and big-eyed-girl paintings. Check them out on the Web at www.glyphs.com/moba.) Otherwise, get your money's worth by looking for the following:

- **Art for art's sake:** Small galleries and regional museums are usually free. They also tend to show work that's more controversial or interactive than your traditional "Old Masters" museum. Look for self-guided gallery tours in your area, or openings where there will be wine and cheese and you can meet the artist. (And look cool doing it.) Who knows? You might just discover the next Picasso.

- **Free day:** Most major museums offer a free or low-cost day. Use your lunch break to work through a room or two every week. Others (like the Met in New York City) are "suggested donation," which means that you can pay whatever you like. For those that have a fixed fee, ask about student admissions. While you're in there, look for other programming—most museums offer guided tours, films, and lectures for the price of admission.

- **Monet by moonlight:** Some city museums open their galleries a few nights a month to the public for cocktails, hors d'oeuvres, music, and dancing.

Arts and Crafts

Are you sick of looking at other people's creations? Make your own masterpieces—alone or with friends.

- **Stuck up:** Buy some magnetic tape and get out a couple of old photographs and some magazines for your own refrigerator magnets. Color with pens, paint, or crayons; lacquer with Modge Podge. The wackier the better.

- **Let there be light:** Have a candle-making party. Buy supplies (molds, wax, tapers, colors, and scents) from a craft store. Decorate with sand, dried flowers, and beads.

- **Look around:** Go out and capture the place where you live—and the people in it—in video, photographs, painting, or drawing.

- **Heavy machinery:** Find a place (check your local university or high school) that has the equipment and space you need for whatever you do, whether it be throwing pots, making furniture, binding books, or soldering jewelry.

- **Hallmark moments:** Make cards with paper scraps, pieces of ribbon, old pictures, and a photocopier. Keep them around for special occasions. Same with scrapbooks—buy an old-fashioned photo album and some photo corners (available at fancy paper stores) and do a little bit every week.

Movie Madness

Drop ten bucks on the latest blockbuster along with everyone else in the country. Collect the action figures from Burger King. Buy the new computer game/cereal combo that's marketed to go along with the film. *Or not.* While there's nothing wrong with enjoying your basic multimillion-dollar star vehicle now and again, there are lots of other ways to enjoy the art of filmmaking.

- **Get celluloid savvy:** Work your way through the classics with friends. Go through certain themes/genres (1950s epics, film noir, documentaries), directors (Fellini, Billy Wilder, Francis Ford Coppola), or actors (Liz Taylor, James Stewart, Al Pacino). Ask for recommendations from friends and family or your local independent video store, or go online for tips.

- **La dolce vita:** Frequent theaters that show independent, foreign, or art films. (Museums sometimes show these types of films as well.) They're the same price or cheaper—beret and cappuccino not included.

- **Make it a matinee:** If you just *have to* go out and see *Scream 7*, see it during the day for half the price, and bring your own candy and bottled soda.

- **Moon-dance:** Not just for Robert Redford anymore. If you've got a few theaters in your town, it's likely there's at least one film festival. It's a great way to see movies that may not normally make it to the big screen, as well as the entire body of work of one filmmaker or actor.

- **Organize a film club:** This is the same idea as a book club, except with movies. And it's a great excuse for massive popcorn consumption.

- **Hooray for Hollywood:** Once you've seen everything, you can get some friends together for an Oscars party. Have everyone dress up and bet on the winners. The person with the worst social life wins.

Music, Theater, Dance, and Performance

If you like your entertainment live, you have lots of lower-cost alternatives to front row center at the latest $100-a-seat extravaganza.

- **Backstage pass:** Volunteer to be an usher at a few of your local performance venues. You get free shows for about an hour's worth of extra work.

- **Lounge lizards:** Live music at concert halls and stadiums is expensive. If you just want a low-key night with some tunes, get it for free or on the cheap at smaller bars and clubs (hotel bars usually have jazz or lounge standards during happy hour). For those into classical or opera, check on tickets for weeknights and matinees, or see if there are any smaller school or conservatory shows. Better yet, learn an instrument and make your own music.

- **All the world's a stage:** When the weather's nice, many city parks and plazas offer free arts programming—not to mention plenty of street performers—on weekends, during the lunch break, and on Friday afternoons. Punch out early and head on over.

- **Master thespian:** Experimental and off-Broadway (or off-off-off-Broadway) theater is often pay-what-you-can or sliding scale (less than twenty bucks). In cities like Chicago, improvisational comedy offers audiences a chance to participate.

- **Let's dance:** Seeing live dance doesn't have to cost too much, especially if it's a small troupe. If you're the do-it-yourself type, pay only the price of admission—and perhaps a one-drink minimum—for clubs and raves (including swing or Latin clubs where there's often dance instruction).

- ***Wilkommen, Bienvenue,* Welcome:** Even if you don't want to spill your guts, going to an open-mic or poetry slam can be a much more moving experience than you'd imagine, as performances usually deal with issues of identity, sexuality, race, class, and culture. San Francisco and New York have great slam cultures, with participants of all ages and ethnicities. For something a little more risqué, check out the drag queen/cabaret scene for an artful rendition of your favorite diva—Madonna, Diana Ross, and Cher every hour, on the hour.

- **Bowling, the ultimate performance art:** Even without the shoes.

Festivals and Fairs

Spring and summer are the big festival seasons, but don't worry, folks will find almost any excuse for a celebration. Festivals come in all shapes and sizes: religious, musical, neighborhood, ethnic. The point? Only to revel, just like the old days, by drinking, dancing, eating, and generally having fun on the cheap. A few of the best:

- **Mardi Gras:** "Fat Tuesday" in February. Do everything to excess (and way beyond) before the beginning of Lent. (Tip: If you want to steer clear of the crowds at New Orleans' Mardi Gras celebration, try another French-heritage city like Mobile, Alabama, or Montreal, Quebec.)

- **Jazz and blues festivals:** Most cities across the country host these types of events throughout the summer. The mother of all music festivals, the New Orleans Jazz and Heritage Festival, kicks 'em off in late April/early May.

- **Pride parades:** As wild as they come, these late-June celebrations are meant to commemorate Stonewall.

- **"Taste of . . ." celebrations:** Usually during the summer, these provide a chance to sample some of your region's best food.

- **Holiday parades:** Cinco de Mayo, Fourth of July, Halloween, Thanksgiving, and such are almost always free—and a whole lot of fun.

- **Fairs, carnivals, amusement parks, and circuses:** Relive your lost youth at a carnival and marvel at its faded charm. The kitschier, the better.

Eat, Drink, and Be Merry

You can always throw your own private festival. Any occasion will do. Hold it in your apartment, in the park, in a restaurant, or at a bar (usually rentable, or you can work out a deal where you collect door fees and the bar makes money on the booze).

- **The irresistible free meal:** Ah, the dinner party. The height of urban sophistication and witty repartee. Set out the Cheetos and pigs-in-a-blanket early.

- **Bring your own steak:** Potlucks are a good way to throw a party and cut down on the expense of buying all that food. Loosely organize who brings what (appetizers, main course, drinks, salad, dessert) and see what turns up. Potluck Sunday brunches are nice, too—don't forget the Bloody Marys and mimosas.

- **Who was that masked man?** Have a theme or costume party for Presidents' Day, Groundhog Day, or your favorite author's birthday. The more bizarre, the better. Tacky parties are always interesting. Dress up and make it a tradition.

- **Up on the rooftop:** If you're hankering for a blowout, get all your neighbors together and collaborate on a block/apartment/roof party. They can be lots of work, but they're worth it.

- **Hootenanny!** Everyone brings an instrument. Too many rhythm guitars—at least ten renditions of "Under the Bridge" and "Patience."

Cooking and Eating

Along with partying, eating is just about everyone's favorite pastime. Most likely you already have a favorite restaurant—besides a meal or two there, shake up your schedule by going on some of these culinary adventures.

- **Table for two:** There's nothing wrong with old standards, but it's good to try out new restaurants every once in a while. How about a few in a night? An appetizer here, a main course there . . . dessert somewhere else.

- **Save some for the ants:** Warm weather? Get your basket and go on a picnic. Frisbee, chess, backgammon, or guitar optional.

- *Bon appétit:* Cooking can actually be *très* enjoyable and very creative (and much less expensive than eating out). Try out a few new recipes with friends. Some gourmet shopping, a little wine, a sauté (cooking quickly in a very hot pan) here, a chiffonade (slicing ribbon-thin) there, a little more wine, and your French is suddenly impeccable!

- **By the glass:** If you're lucky to live in a wine-producing area, spend an afternoon or weekend visiting vineyards and tasting the goods. (Or you can buy a couple of bottles and do the same thing at home with some friends.) Not only do you learn something, but you also get to say things like "delicate nose" and "buttery undertones." If you're the beer type, look for a nearby microbrewery.

- **Gone pickin':** If you're near an agricultural area, summer and fall are the perfect time to pick fruit and make pies or jelly.

You'll find apples and other orchard fruit in New England, berries in California, the Northwest, and the Midwest.

Shopping

This kind of shopping is more about the looking than the buying. Warning: Making a whole day of shopping without emptying your bank account requires willpower and resolve—and very eclectic taste. Not for the fainthearted.

- **E-I-E-I-O:** Go for a drive and stop at farmers' markets. Eat your goods along the way, or cook what you buy when you get home.

- **4-sale:** Garage-saling and antiquing are a good excuse to walk or drive around the neighborhood. (Plus it's fun to rifle through someone else's stuff.) If you want more bang for your buck, start a collection—1950s kitchen aprons, lunch boxes, old tools, etc. It makes all that tramping around even more enjoyable.

- **Window shop:** That's the reason they have windows, after all. Try on expensive designer clothes, sit on thousand-dollar chairs. Get yourself a makeover at the makeup counter and collect samples. *Just don't buy anything.* If you're good, treat yourself to a bunch of flowers when you're done.

- *Domo arigato*: Shop in ethnic stores. It's usually cheaper and always more interesting. Buy a sari from an Indian silk store, incense and paper lanterns in Chinatown, or origami paper or fancy chopsticks from a Japanese dry goods store.

Visiting

Even when you're busy, an afternoon or evening spent with a friend or relative is more than entertaining—it's downright therapeutic.

- **Wisdom of the ages:** Get to know some older folks and hang out with them once in a while. If you've got a video or tape recorder, you might even start an oral history so as to keep their memories alive.

- **Terrible twenties:** Miss having children around? Babysit for someone. It's excellent birth control, plus you get to act like a kid for a few hours.

- **Like a virgin:** Used clothes that seem new! Have a bitch-n-swap night with your friends. Get a big bottle of wine, listen to Madonna (guys can substitute Frank Sinatra or something), and trade old clothes. Give the rest to the Salvation Army.

Quiet Time

Remember that your twenties are also a time for introspection—soul searching, even—and you'll need a few times a week when it's just you and no one else. Anyway, after the party's over, you'll probably crave a free moment or two. What to do when you're flying solo:

- **Read:** Hey, you're doing it right now! Short stories in bed, the Sunday paper on the stoop, *Sports Illustrated* on the . . . you get the picture. Buy your books at a local used bookstore, or pick them up for twenty-five cents at yard and sidewalk sales. Remember the library? You can usually get a card for less than a dollar, and it's free in many big cities.

- **People-watch:** Make up stories about the folks you see in the park, at the bus station, in the bathroom mirror in the morning.

- **Meander:** Take a walk, ride a train or bus to a new place, and see what you see. If you're not too creeped out, graveyards are actually nice to walk in. Look at the old names—very quiet and calm.

- **Browse:** Stroll down to your local music or bookstore to read the magazines and listen to CDs for free.

- **Pet:** Getting nostalgic for the old family dog/cat/ferret/turtle? Head on over to your nearest pet shop and spend a little time oohing and aahing at the puppies and kittens. Resist the urge to take one home with you.

- **List:** Make a list of all the things you want to do in your life. Go back to it every few years to add to it, as well as see how much you've accomplished.

- **Sleuth:** Get on the Internet and do some genealogical research about your family. The Church of Latter-day Saints' genealogical site, Family Search, is a good place to start (www.familysearch.com). Or visit your local historical society; look through old newspapers and marvel at how much—or little—things have changed.

- **Worship:** Haven't been to church, temple, or synagogue in a while? Drop in one Sunday (or Saturday) for a couple of hours.

- **Meditate:** Cultivate your inner Buddha. Anytime, anyplace.

- **Treat yourself:** Nail salons can sometimes function as spas-for-less. Besides doing manicures and pedicures (for men, too!), they'll often give facials and mini-massages—for about a quarter of what a day spa will run you. If you've got an extra sixty bucks, an hour massage is certainly worth the money. If not, trade massages with a friend (platonically, of course) or lover (definitely *not* platonically!).

- **Figure out the rest of your life:** Get your astrological chart done—either by an expert (about seventy-five dollars) or for free on the Internet (www.astrology.com—look under "Chart Shop"). Visit a palm or tarot reader for fun. Make them bust out the crystal ball.

The Singles Thing

Okay, okay, enough quality time with yourself already. If you're sick of hanging out alone and want to meet new friends—or perhaps someone special—there's a lot you can do. Simply getting out is one way to meet people (it's hard to socialize when you're alone in your apartment). So is asking your friends to set you up, taking a class, or doing any one of the number of social options listed above. Should your angling still not catch you a beau or belle, fear not—there's an entire *industry* dedicated to finding you a mate.

- **Matchmaker, matchmaker, make me a match:** Look in the paper or online for singles parties, dating services, etc. Most of them are pretty cheesy, but as the old saying goes . . . you never know until you try. Some religious and affinity organizations have gatherings that subtly cater to singles (no name tags required). You may want to start there.

- **Let's get personal:** Depending on where you live, the personal ads in your local newspaper or alternative weekly will vary in "normalness" and quality. In Chicago, people use the *Reader*'s listings all the time. Opt for a regular mailbox rather than voicemail, if the option is available. Even if you're not going to actually answer them, the letters are fun to read.

Vice

There's nothing wrong with a little vice taken in small measure—just make sure you know when to stop. And while it's always an option, you may want to try one or two healthier pursuits before you head off to the bars.

- **Behind the eight-ball:** Pool is certainly one of the most in-nocuous of the traditional vices. Darts, too. Play alone or in a group. You can have hours of fun for a few quarters. Or, if you're particularly good, you can make a few bucks hustling.

- **Off to the races:** You don't have to risk a lot at the horse and dog tracks—heck, you don't have to bet at all, though it makes the running a little more exciting if you do. People-watching at these events can be terrific entertainment, although probably not if you're an animal-rights type.

- **Gambling fever:** We all know how long a few hundred bucks will last you at blackjack. My advice? Stay at the nickel slots. And if you absolutely *must* play blackjack, always double-down on 11 (unless the dealer has an ace) and never take insurance (except the real-life kind).

- **Where everybody knows your name:** Bars—while being the second home to millions of alcoholics nationwide—can provide a kind of community, too, especially if it's a neighborhood hangout. Try local places where you can meet people and talk to the bartender.

- **Poker night:** Penny/dime poker (or gin, or mah-jongg, or crazy eights) is cheap and fun, especially if you have a regular meeting night each month.

- **BINGO!** Need we say more?

Travel

Finally, if you can't find *anything* to do around town, you can always strap on your backpack and take off for a few days/weeks/months/years. If you've got a car, great. If not, there's always Greyhound. More on traveling in Chapter 14, but in the meantime:

- **B&B:** Consider a weekend in the country. In the off-season, rates can be as little as thirty to forty dollars a night, with a *way* better breakfast than you'd make at home.

- **Get away without leaving town:** No money for a trip? Be a tourist in your own city. Climb the highest building. Go on a walking tour. Visit historical sites. Walk along the waterfront (if you have one) or ride a ferry (ditto). Call it a day by buying some cheap postcards. Send one to your best friend from home, your oldest friend, and your grandma.

- **Back on the bus:** Visit friends in another city for the weekend. Go home for your mom's lasagna. Whatever your pleasure, bus travel in the continental U.S. is still the cheapest way to get around. Greyhound offers a Student Advantage card that gets you discounts on bus fares nationwide (www.studentadvantage.com, 800-333-2920). If you're in the West, try Green Tortoise (www.greentortoise.com, 800-TORTOISE.) the famous "alternative" bus line (no seats, a stop at hot springs on the ride from Portland to San Francisco). They also take a spring break trip to Costa Rica for those in the mood for a longer trip.

- **Fly Away:** Airlines and travel agencies are always offering weekend packages on the cheap. Look for consolidators in the newspaper. Airline companies usually have special Web fares at the last minute if you're flexible. Check the major carriers' websites, as well as cheap ticket purveyors Cheap Tickets (www.cheaptickets.com), Lowestfare.com (www.lowestfare.com), and Priceline.com (www.priceline.com).

CHAPTER 7

On the Cheap

So you've taken our advice in the housing, food, financial, and entertainment areas and you're *still* coming up short. Give up and start putting the rest on your credit card? *No!* You just need to start making some changes in your basic spending habits. Here's how.

First rule of enlightened frugality: Getting something *on the cheap* is not the same thing as *being cheap*. Being cheap implies a desire to cut corners as well as costs, a privileging of price over quality, and, sometimes, a basic lack of good taste. Frugality (or thrift, or simple living, or whatever you want to call it), on the other hand, is about valuing your life and spending time doing what *you* want to rather than what *your job* dictates. (You've got to give up a lot of hours to sustain a serious spending habit. Remember how many work hours any given purchase costs you next time you cough up the dough.)

Being frugal requires extra creativity, a little effort and patience, some consumer know-how, and lots of solid decision-making (i.e., when to spend a penny to save a buck). As author Amy Dacyczyn of the famous *Tightwad Gazette* series puts it, "There is a point at which the quality of life and the standard of living depart . . . where earning more results in a personal cost and erodes the quality of life. The solution is to find the right balance of earning more and saving more." (Every issue of Dacyczyn's *Tightwad Gazette* newsletters is available in one giant frugal extravaganza: *The Complete Tightwad Gazette,* Villard, 1998.)

Frugal Tips

So if you're into frugality for the long haul—or as a "viable alternative lifestyle," as Dacyczyn calls it—here are a few pages of helpful hints, organized by category, to get you going. Try one or all and see where you save the most.

Note: Much more information than we can offer here is available in Dacyczyn's book, as well as on websites like The Dollar Stretcher (www.stretcher.com) and www.tightwad.com.

Food and Cooking

- Spend some time planning meals to avoid more expensive impulse buys at the grocery store.

- If you're a tap water snob, instead of always buying your water in jugs or bottles, invest in a filtered water pitcher. It'll run you about $20, plus $7 for a new filter.

- The better part of all kitchen work can be accomplished with a single 8-inch chef's knife and a good paring knife. At nonsale retail prices, a good knife is about $35 to $55 for the chef's knife and often less than $10 for the paring knife. Another good source for kitchen knives is a large Asian foods market—they'll have Chinese cleavers for about $15 or so. If you combine these purchases with a good sharpening steel/stone and use it, your knives will last longer than you will! (Not to be morbid or anything.)

- If you keep bananas in a closed bag, they will keep at least two weeks on your counter (compared to one week for uncovered bananas).

- Put an apple in a bag of potatoes to keep the potatoes from sprouting and wrinkling. This works for up to eight weeks.

- Save vegetable leavings—e.g., carrot peels, onion skins, and celery leaves—in a plastic bag in the freezer. Boil down with chicken or turkey bones, salt, pepper, and herbs to make yummy, fresh soup stock. It's much better than those little cubes, and freezable.

- If you can stand any more of it, right *after* Thanksgiving is a good time to get your turkey (about $0.50 per pound).

- Instead of expensive juice or soda, try iced black or herbal teas unsweetened or with a little honey. Red zinger or cranberry cove work especially well in lieu of cranberry juice. Try green tea (lots of antioxidants), peppermint tea, or fruity black teas for variety. A $3.50 box makes about fifteen pitchers.

- Sprouts for health! For learning! For fun! Did you know that sprouts are pretty much the healthiest food you can eat? Toss 'em on salads, sandwiches, and stir-fries and watch your muscles grow! (Okay, maybe not, but they are healthy—and *cheap* if you learn how to make them at home.)

- If you've got a sunny window or porch (or, even better, a garden), you can grow and dry your own herbs in pots for winter use or convenience. (Plus, in the summer, nothing beats fresh basil.) Mint, chives, parsley, basil, oregano, rosemary, thyme, and chili peppers all grow well in pots. Herbs can be grown from seed in early spring or bought already potted. To dry, bundle eight to ten stems with a rubber band and hang upside down in a well-circulated area out of direct sunlight. In a week or so, check the leaves to see if they are crispy. If they are, remove the leaves from the stem, crush, put into a lidded container, label, and store out of direct sunlight.

- Constantly throwing out milk? If you can get used to the taste, buy your milk powdered or in vacuum boxes to avoid spoilage.

- If you drink alcohol, buy in bulk. Packaging adds most of the cost to liquor products.

How to Sprout Sprouts

Put seeds or beans (sunflower, pumpkin, alfalfa, barley, garbanzo, wheat, kidney, lima, soy, etc.) in a quart jar—2 tablespoons for small seeds like alfalfa or clover, $\frac{1}{2}$ cup for beans or grains. Beans should be rinsed thoroughly and not overcrowded in the jar. Cover with three or four times as much water as seeds.

After soaking seeds for eight to twelve hours, place a piece of nylon net or fiberglass window screen over the top of the jar. Secure it with a jar ring or wide elastic band. Pour off the water (which contains nutrients, so save it for making soups or to water your plants) and rinse seeds well with lukewarm water.

When no water drips from seeds, roll jar so that most seeds coat sides of jar. Then lay jar on its side in a warm (about 70 degrees), dark place and rinse sprouts with lukewarm water twice a day (or just often enough to keep moist for alfalfa or clover) until sprouts have reached the desired length (two to five days).

Most failures occur because sprouts sour and mold if they are too wet. For better drainage, drain for up to a half-hour with the jar tilted.

- Never shop for food when you're hungry, unless you want to come home loaded with HoHos and chips.

- Make sure you compare the cost of bulk food with the packaged stuff at your local supermarket. Supermarkets have gotten wise to the "romantic" experience of buying bulk and will often charge you more for bulk than large packages of generic brands. Bigger packaging does not always mean cheaper—always compare price per ounce.

- When you're out shopping, stock up when you find a good price on a favorite or staple item.

Guacamole
Makes about 1 cup:
Salt
1   clove garlic
1   large ripe avocado, pitted
$\frac{1}{4}$ teaspoon chili powder
1   teaspoon lime juice
2   teaspoons minced onion
Mash all ingredients together. Serve with chips.

Shopping

Bargain everywhere you go, even at retail shops. Tips for haggling success:

- If anything is wrong with the item—*anything*, from loose threads to a jammed zipper or a paint scratch—ask to see the manager. They may take a couple of bucks off, depending on the store's reputation, the quality of the item, and its price.

- If the season is changing, try this one: "The weather's getting too cold for air conditioners, and I see this is your last one. How about a little discount?"

- Offer to pay cash for big-ticket items and name your price. Either they'll take it or they won't. Doesn't hurt to try.

- Find the lowest available price on a given make and model and then see if another place will match the price. If you're after a computer, check with New York City computer retailers first. Because of the high sales tax, they're forced to sell their models at rock-bottom prices. Then go to your local store or computer warehouse and see if they'll match or beat it.

- If an item you recently purchased goes on sale, take your receipt to the manager. Many stores will refund you the difference.

- Do not, under any circumstances, fail to haggle with sidewalk vendors, thrift stores, pawnbrokers (or any other kind of used-merchandise seller), car salespeople, and jewelers.

Transportation

- Learn how to change your own oil and perform other simple car maintenance procedures.

- If frugality is truly important to you, *never ever ever* buy a new car. If you must have a very shiny car, check first with the rental car companies. They usually sell low-mileage cars (under 20,000 miles) at lower than the blue book value.

- If you just *have* to have a new one, at least shop for it at the end of the month. The dealer will be less worried about covering monthly overhead and more interested in moving 'em out fast so as to avoid interest on the borrowed inventory. It's also possible that salespeople participate in a bonus plan based on the number of sales made in a month. If they've made their quota, they're less likely to quibble over a lower commission.

- Get in just before closing, when salespeople are more ready to make a deal—your trade-in might just get a once-over.

- Shop in September and October for savings on end-of-model-year cars.

Household

- All-purpose cleaning solution: $\frac{1}{2}$ cup of ammonia, $\frac{1}{3}$ cup of vinegar, 2 tablespoons of baking soda, and 1 gallon of water.

- A cheap alternative to Windex: plain old vinegar and water (a half-and-half solution), wiped down with newspaper. Try not to clean in direct sunlight, as it causes the windows to dry too quickly, leaving streaks. This concoction is great for shining windows and fixtures (but not good on wood).

- Place a small amount of bleach in a spray bottle and fill it with water. Keep it by the bathtub to get rid of mildew, and use it to clean countertops and wipe down bathroom counters and toilet seats.

- Use rubbing alcohol to clean bathroom and kitchen fixtures. It makes them shiny and spotfree!

- Got a clogged drain? The plumber's secret recipe (which might not work for *really* bad clogs): Pour at least a cup of bleach down the drain, and immediately follow with a pot of boiling water. Bend one end of a wire hanger over to make it easier to grasp. Bend the other end into as small a hook as you can. Stick the thing down the drain hole, little hook end first, as far as you can, and pull it out. Repeat. Each time you will pull out huge chunks of matted hair. (Mmmm!) The water will drain much smoother afterward! This method is cheaper and less toxic than commercial drain cleaners.

- In your search for a frugal cleaner, *do not* under any circumstances mix bleach with ammonia. The chemical reaction releases a poisonous gas that, combined with an ill-ventilated bathroom, could be lethal.

- Ah, nothing like mold in the morning! After a certain point, even your shower curtain needs a bath. Instead of getting a new one, put it in the washing machine with two towels, $\frac{1}{2}$ cup of detergent, and $\frac{1}{2}$ cup of baking soda. During the last rinse cycle, add another $\frac{1}{2}$ cup of vinegar. Hang immediately to discourage wrinkles.

- For really nasty pans, add automatic dishwasher detergent to the water and soak it for twenty minutes. Even the toughest spaghetti gunk practically slides off.

- Stuff plastic grocery bags into an old facial tissue box. When you need one to line your bathroom wastebasket (or, even better, to carry back to the grocery store the next time you shop), simply pull one out. The rest stay neatly in the box.

- Don't buy paper towels or paper napkins. Invest in some cloth napkins—much classier, anyway—and use rags for cleaning. Not only is this less expensive, but you're saving trees and minimizing trash buildups at the same time.

- Swiffer made simple: Dryer sheets make great dusters, especially for furniture that gathers dust easily, like blinds and computer monitors. It adds a fresh smell, too! Use tape to stick a few sheets onto the end of a broom/mop, and you have an extendable version for higher/lower spots. When you're finished, put the sheets in the bottom of your garbage can to help get rid of odors.

- Last night's party left a couple of stains? Blot up (don't rub) as much of the liquid/ash/dirt/um . . . *regurgitant*? as possible. Apply dish detergent mixed with cool water. If it's still there, try some white vinegar, dabbing the area with a towel. Rinse and dry and see if it's gone. If it's not, try color-safe bleach. If everything else fails, put a potted plant over the spot and chalk it up to merrymaking.

- A little wine, a little music, a little kootchy-koo . . . and you forgot to blow out all those candles. Now there's wax everywhere and what's-his/her-name is long gone. How do you get wax out of your cozy carpet without spending a fortune at the rug cleaner? First, pick away whatever pieces you can. Cover the rest with a thin cotton towel, a sheet of tin foil, and another thin towel. Heat the iron to high and place it on the top of the towel/foil thingy. The heat will melt the wax, and the pressure of the iron will draw the wax into the towel. If your rug is synthetic, this will still work, but be sure to remove the iron before it melts the fibers. This procedure also works with clothes, but again, beware of burning if they're delicate. Repeat until all traces of the night are removed.

- For pen stains in cotton/polyester, spray the spot with a hair spray that contains alcohol to dissolve the ink. Plain rubbing alcohol will also work, as long as it is *isopropyl* alcohol, not tequila or 151 proof, please.

Personal Care

- Make your own leave-in conditioner by mixing one part regular conditioner to five parts water. Put it in an empty hair-spray container and spritz it on, or leave the mix in the conditioner bottle and run it through wet hair.

- Use hair conditioner or the cheapest combination shampoo/conditioner as an alternative to expensive shaving cream. Works great and costs half as much in the long run.

- Frugal facial: Steam your face with a hot towel infused with lemon or peppermint. (Boil water with the juice of one lemon, fresh peppermint leaves, or, in a pinch, a peppermint tea bag.) Let it cool a little before you dip the towel in it.

- Egg on your face! If you just happen to be using raw eggs for cooking, there's a film on the inside of the shell that can be applied to "problem areas" of your face as a natural mask. Let it dry and don't forget to peel it off before company comes.

- Witch hazel is a low-cost alternative to over-the-counter astringent. It can help bring the swelling down for sprains and bruises, too.

- Blemish relief: A bit of calamine lotion or toothpaste dabbed on before bed dries that zit right up.

- Best thing for dry skin? Rub in a generic olive oil (without the garlic flavoring, please) after a shower while you're still a little wet. Pure coconut or almond oil works well, too, though these can cause clogged pores. For serious moisturizing, try pure vitamin E oil around the eyes (and other wrinkly places) at night. All are usually available at your local health food store.

- For a hangover headache cure, cut a lime in half and rub it on your forehead. The throbbing will go away and you'll smell like a margarita! (Or maybe that's not such a good thing.)

- If you're willing to take a chance, check out your local beauty school or salon training center for cheaper prices on cuts and coloring. Salon training centers are better for those who want a "whole new you" (the cuts can sometimes be, shall we say, *experimental*). Schools more often cater to folks who just want a basic trim.

- Pick up free condoms at Planned Parenthood or your local health center.

Clothing

- Dry clean only? Perhaps not. Hand washing—with just a little gentle soap and cold water—works on most sweaters, silks, and rayon. (Not so with suit jackets or wedding dresses!) Hang up or lay flat to dry, away from heat that will cause shrinkage. Always test a nonshowing piece of the fabric before you wash the whole thing.

- Take old clothes to a consignment shop first—they'll give you half of whatever they sell and donate the rest to charity. Better than a yard sale (or a garbage bag).

- Try a flea comb (available at most pet stores) to get rid of those annoying fuzzballs on sweaters (especially cashmere), blankets, and mattresses. Better than an electric shaver, which needs batteries and often clogs up. Go easy on sweater fabrics, holding the comb nearly flat to the sweater surface and going slowly.

- Wash brightly colored clothes (like those dark denim jeans) inside-out in cold water. Color stays longer, and you may save a little on your water heating bill.

The Three Rs: Reduce, Reuse, and Recycle

- Don't let the water run while you are washing your hands or brushing your teeth.

- Take short showers whenever possible.

- Turn off all lights and appliances when not in use. (Duh.)

- Recycle! Computer paper makes good next-to-the-phone message pads, and tin foil is just as protective the second time around (ditto with Ziploc bags). Use old clothes for polishing shoes or dusting, old yogurt containers as Tupperware. The list goes on and on . . . and on.

- Create an e-mail list called "Reuse." Let folks know what you're trying to get rid of, and most likely, it'll be gone in a few days. If it isn't, leave it out by the Dumpster—in a box or on the side so people know it's the "treasure" kind of trash.

- If you live near a university, check out what gets left behind a day or two after the students leave. There are enough couches, clothes, and mini-fridges to stock a small hotel. Make sure to keep your probing out by the Dumpster, however. If you're not a student, officials won't take too kindly to your roaming the halls.

Miscellaneous

- Try buying (and selling) your music (and other assorted junk) on eBay.com or one of the other online bidding sites. New CDs can be bought for two to five dollars plus shipping. (Plus, you're helping folks clean out their closets!) You can find designer clothing there cheap, too—usually 50 percent off.

- Get your film and prints by mail. It's cheaper than at the drugstore. Try York Labs at www.yorklabs.com.

- If you qualify, get yourself an International Student Identity card, available from Council Travel (800-333-2920) or STA (800-781-4040). It works in the U.S. and abroad to get you discounts on everything from transportation to museum entrance fees to hostel stays. They're good for only one year, so make sure that you can justify the twenty-dollar price tag.

- Look for value-added vacation packages to get goodies like a free car, a third night free at the hotel, airport pickup, and complementary lei (the flower kind).

- Set aside 1 percent of every paycheck for pure pleasure; that way you don't have to feel guilty when you splurge on some nonessential joy.

- Looking to get something for nothing? Try TheFreeSite.com for freebie listings by category.

CHAPTER 8

Starting
Early

Now that you've got the basics of survival *down*—you're situated, you've paid the phone bill, you know the difference between an HMO and a PPO—you're ready to revisit where we left off in chapter 2. Despite your new competency with homemade cleaning solutions and rental insurance, the question remains:

So whaddya gonna do with the rest of your life?

If you don't know the answer, don't worry. No one really knows what they're going to do with the rest of their life; they just pretend they do. But by now you should at least be thinking about where you want to be for the next few months or years, workwise. In other words, it's time to get a J-O-B.

The next few chapters should get you started on the process, but if you're angling for a more in-depth look at the job search, there are a few books devoted entirely to helping you become gainfully employed. Check out *Guide to Your Career* or *The Internship Bible*—both brought to you by The Princeton Review— or check the major online employment sites. They usually have a few pages devoted to job search how-to's.

Working 9 to 5 (You Wish)

More like 8:30 to 6, with a half-hour or so to gobble down lunch. Figure on an hour or so on each side to get ready and/or wind down, plus your commute, and you're looking at about a 12-hour workday. That's 60 hours a week devoted to your work—240 hours a month, 12,000 hours a year. Not to mention the time you spend talking, worrying, and dreaming about what you do. *Gulp!*

The point of all the number-crunching? Considering how much time you're going to spend at this J-O-B for the next couple of months . . . years . . . decades, it's a good idea to take the extra time *now* to find something you actually like to do. Which means, of course, starting early.

Starting Early Is a State of Mind

If you're like most of us, you may have started preparing for this moment in kindergarten—remember the lemonade stand?—but *still* be convinced you are late. You're not. So you didn't get that resume-building internship your last year of college. Why not see if there's one available now? So you bummed around Europe this summer instead of taking that job that started in June. Good. You'll have the rest of your life to work, but precious little of it to see the world.

Feeling late breeds panic, and panic makes you rush into things. *Don't.* Consider everything that you've done before today as preparation for the only moment that really matters: now. Take a second to listen to what your heart wants. If you don't have strong feelings in any particular direction, all right—let fate take you where it will. Some people *do* stumble into rewarding careers pretty much by accident. (However, many more just don't take the time or have the courage to do what they really want to do and end up staying in their jobs primarily because they feel they have to.) But if you have even the slightest inkling that you were meant to be a florist/astronaut/chef/etc., you owe it to yourself to check it out.

> **Show Some Initiative**
>
> **Fred Bernstein** decided not to wait until after he graduated from Princeton to begin pursuing his career in journalism. All through college he wrote campus-related freelance articles for a local newspaper. When he graduated, the newspaper immediately offered him a full-time job.
>
> "Let's put it this way," Fred advises. "If you want to be a journalist and Henry Kissinger comes to speak at your college, write a story and send it out immediately to your local newspaper."

Okay, so maybe it isn't so easy to just "check out" being a neurosurgeon or a famous Hollywood actress. But you've got to start somewhere, and you've got to do it without delay—*whenever* you start. In other words, as soon as you have an idea where you want to end up, you've got to begin heading toward it. What matters isn't so much *when* as what your attitude is when you set off. Keep your eyes on the prize and you'll end up winning it.

It's pretty simple: To get an interesting job in a field that you love, you have to be able to offer your employers something that they want. The good news? Whether you know it or not, you already have a lot going for you—youth, optimism, fresh ideas, and a willingness to work hard (not to mention a willingness to work for a lot less money than that middle manager with a wife, three kids, and a pension). And while these go a long way to getting you in the door, there's one little thing you may or may not be missing. It's called *experience*, and it's what that middle manager has a whole lot of.

Lucky for you, young whipper-snapper, there are two surefire ways to get experience, even in fields that are notoriously hard to break into. Number one? Volunteer work. Number two? Internships. And for those of you who think that you've got to be independently wealthy to afford one of these instead of a real (read: *paying*) job, think again. We'll show you strategies for breaking into the job of your dreams while still putting food on the table (and beer in the fridge).

Internships and Volunteer Work

Every year, companies all across the United States and around the world hire college students and post-college young people to work in their organizations as interns or volunteers. While some internships do offer some compensation—usually a monthly or term stipend that helps with living expenses or, in some cases, free room and board—many are unpaid. Think of it as a kind of apprenticeship to the field. You give a couple of months, and they give you an entrance to the trade of your choice by way of three all-important qualifications for future employment: something to put on your resume, actual on-the-job experience, and a professional recommendation. (Some internships also earn you college credit, a boon if you're reading this while still in school.)

While you're probably familiar with internships in law firms, investment banking companies, and Congress (and, of course, the White House), internships and volunteer work can take many shapes and forms. Yours doesn't necessarily have to be run through a program or found through your school's career counseling center, though these avenues may give you a leg up on the competition. Internships can range from serving as a photographer's assistant in Boston to studying river fish in a United States Forest Service outpost in Colorado to teaching English in Tokyo. Whatever your goals and geographic preferences, the type of internship/volunteer job you can get is limited only by your imagination (and your funds, but we'll get to that later).

Best of all, besides providing you with a resume boost, volunteer/internship work gives you the opportunity to find out whether you actually enjoy the day-to-day life of, say, a Spanish bullfighter (upside: admiration of millions, lots of excitement, good coffee, a fancy outfit; downside: bulls). If you've ever asked yourself, "What would it be like to work on a political campaign?" you can find out—just like Emily McDermott did after she finished her Master's in Social Work at the University of Chicago. Keen to exercise her democratic rights, Emily volunteered for an Illinois state rep's campaign. When she saw the political process from the inside—which evidently involves huge quantities of doughnuts and coffee—she realized she liked effecting change behind the scenes, pounding the pavement seven days a week for votes. So now she now works for the Feds as a program analyst for Health and Human Services and drives a beige, late-model Buick and wears mirrored aviator sunglasses, just like she's always wanted. (Just kidding, Emily.)

How to Find One

If you're still in school or recently graduated, the first place to look for an internship or volunteer job is at your college's career center. There they've got internship/volunteer work listings from all over the place—companies that are interested in applicants from your school. Just going to one particular university can give you an edge over the competition, so start here when you're looking for that perfect entry into your chosen field.

And if you're done with school and worried that you didn't do the internship thing while you were still in college? No sweat. Even if you're a few years out, don't be shy about using the resources your school's career center offers. They have information for both students *and* alumni, as well as counselors that can assist both types of job seekers. Moreover, many of the "college-only" listings are open to folks who are just out of school. Look under the job's eligibility requirements, or give them a call. Mostly, employers want warm bodies that can think. Applicants a little bit older might even have a better shot because they'll be viewed as more mature and, of course, more experienced.

In addition to looking through the listings at your career center, it's crucial to network—including with your own friends and family—asking around about the kind of job you want.

A Becoming Telephone Personality

Shannon Hudnall had been doing a part-time internship at a government agency during her senior year at Georgetown in Washington, D.C. "It was just supposed to be a filing-and-fetching-coffee sort of job," Shannon explains, "but I decided to really go for it. So I did a lot of things that weren't part of the job description." The result? Shannon made a great impression and was offered a temporary job after she graduated.

"So then I happened to be talking on the telephone with a man from an international trade consulting firm whom I'd dealt with during my internship. I knew he thought I'd done well at the internship, so I asked him if he had heard of any jobs, since all I had was a temporary job. He called back in two minutes, and said yes, he did know of a job. I'm starting this Monday."

Personal recommendations go a long way to finding the right fit between employer and employee, and the more people you've got working on your particular case, the better. Eric Meyer's first internship with a lobbyist in Hartford, Connecticut, came as a suggestion from his mom, herself a lobbyist. Pam Green found her first job as an agent's assistant through her best friend, whose father was a top literary agent in L.A.

Finally, there are several books that list thousands of internships all around the world. The best and most up-to-date (all right, all right, just one more plug) are The Princeton Review's *Best 106 Internships* and *The Internship Bible*.

What They're Looking For

The bad news is that internships and volunteer jobs—just like any other job— look for experience first. Considering the fact that you're applying for an internship precisely because you want to *get* experience, the whole thing may seem like a rather cruel catch-22 designed to frustrate aspiring applicants.

The good news is that you probably already have lots of experience; you just have to learn how to look at it in the right way. Chapter 10 has lots of helpful hints on how to use summer jobs, extracurricular activities, and relevant course work for maximum impact on your resume.

As for grades, while a good academic record is essential for certain types of internships—often in the science, engineering, law, or financial fields—jobs in other industries, such as communications or publishing, are more likely to look for related course work and solid interest/expertise in the field. In other words, don't be afraid to apply for an internship just because you've got a couple of Cs on your transcript.

How to Apply

Remember that you are competing against millions of other short-term applicants looking for internship jobs, so the best time to apply for these is usually several months in advance—as early as December for a start date of late May or early June. Many internship deadlines are rolling, so the earlier you start, the better.

Remember, too, that some of the more plum internships—especially those that pay—can receive a thousand applications for a handful of spots. To land one of these sought-after positions, you'll want to find a way to distinguish yourself from your peers, many of whom have similar qualifications. Again, look in chapter 10 for ways to make your resume and cover letter stand out from the rest.

The first rule of getting noticed, however, is simply to make sure your application gets directed to a specific person rather than the company at large. Each internship/ volunteer listing, whether you found it in your college career center, in a guidebook, or through a family friend, should contain the name of a contact person to whom you will be sending your credentials. Two weeks after you've sent your stuff, follow up with a phone call to that person. If you don't hear back from them, try again in a few days—most likely your prospective employer was busy at the moment you called and your (gentle) persistence will be looked upon favorably as a sign of your determination and sincere interest in the job.

When you call, try to have a few questions already written down in front of you—either regarding the application process ("Is there any other information you need?" or "Would you like me to call you next week?") or the job itself ("I'm particularly interested in content management, and I read that the job would entail some hands-on digital editing work—could you tell me more about that aspect of the internship?"). Make sure you're respectful of their time, saying, for instance, "I have a few questions to ask about the internship—is now a good time, or should I make an appointment to call back?" You could also offer to e-mail a few questions as an alternative to calling back. You may find yourself being interviewed over the phone right then and there. Be ready for this possibility by doing as much research as possible about the company and the job *before* you call.

Most likely, however, if an employer is interested in you, they'll get in touch within a few weeks of receiving your resume to set up a face-to-face (or phone, if you're far away) interview. While this interview will be pretty much identical to one you'd have for a regular job (see chapter 10), there's a few things we should mention now.

The Interview

As with any interview, you're going to want to be prepared for the meeting. This means putting on your best duds, getting enough sleep the night before, and—this is crucial—arriving at your interview at least ten minutes early. (Arrive late and you've already got one strike against you.) Preparation also means getting to know the place where you're interviewing. The company probably has a website, and checking it out should be your first step. Also, if you've found the job through your career center, they most likely have a folder with more information on the company. Then check on the Internet or at the public library for recent newspaper or magazine articles written about the company. Familiarize yourself with the company's image—at least on paper—and its products/services. Spend a little time thinking of good, specific questions to ask your interviewer—questions that show that you are actually interested in the company you'd be working for, not just another kid looking for something to put on your resume.

> ### Would You Stop with the Offers Already?
>
> **Gwen Smith** had targeted the hotel industry for quite a while. In her junior year she did a summer internship with Marriott. During her senior year she was selected for a recruitment interview with another Marriott division: "They offered me the job *during* the interview. It was very unusual. I don't know what happened." Just for practice, she went on a few more interviews with other hotel companies, "but it was just for fun. I wanted the job at Marriott."

This goes for the nature of the work you'll be doing, as well. Don't hesitate to ask questions about what a typical day might look like, how many hours a week they'll be needing help, and who you'll be working with (and under). If the person interviewing you isn't going to be that person, try to get a chance to meet your potential boss.

Internships can be less defined than regular jobs, so it's important, even at this early stage, to get a good idea of what you can expect and what will be expected of you. Does the job sound like mostly busywork? Ask about how you might fashion a few independent projects to take on more responsibility. Are you going to be saddled with more work than your twenty-hour commitment can bear? See about the possibility of your internship turning into a full-time job somewhere in the near future. Look around the office to get a sense of its pace and environment. Does this look like a place where you'd want to work? Remember that this meeting is as much for you as for them, and plan your questions (and responses) accordingly.

Finally, don't be alarmed if you're not offered the job right there on the spot. Even if they love you, they're likely to run through the rest of their roster, if only for protocol's sake. Plus, this can give you a few days to decide what you'll say if you get the call. Of course, a note thanking them (along with a reminder of how they can contact you) is a requirement, no matter how well—or badly— you thought the interview went. You never know when you may cross paths again, and you'll be glad you left them with a good impression.

The Job Itself

Unless you're fantastically lucky, getting an internship means that for the next couple of months, you're going to be working hard for little or no money. You're also going to be doing a lot of routine, boring tasks that—you guessed it—no one else in the company wants to do. You might get frustrated with your coworkers, who seem to be oblivious to the fact that there's a better, more efficient way to do just about everything, if they'd just *ask* you. And you also might be jealous of your superiors, who always seem to be (a) going to lunch, (b) sitting in meetings where they also eat lunch (nice roast beef sandwiches and Pellegrino), or (c) ordering lunch, brought by you into their cushy, many-windowed offices. These are the realities of internship life. Stay long enough, and maybe someday you'll have an intern of your own to order around.

Aye, there's the rub. As mundane as that pesky filing is, the experience you're getting will indeed take you to the next level. Remember, there's no law against offering to take on a few more challenging projects *in addition* to your boring tasks. While some internships are highly regimented and pre-planned, most fall under the heading of "You take from it what you make it." Don't be afraid to talk to your boss or coworkers if you feel you're being under- or over-utilized. Most likely, they'll appreciate the feedback. You might even think about creating an "internship handbook" to help the folks who'll come after you get the most out of their job.

How long does an internship/volunteer gig last? A month or two is usually the minimum amount of time it takes to get some meaningful work done after your initial orientation. If you're there after six months, still slogging away for nothing but the sheer adventure of it, consider yourself sufficiently trained to move on to a paying job. And don't be afraid to look for other work if the first thing you try just doesn't work out.

The Money Gig

For many of us—whether in school or graduated—a nonpaying internship or volunteer job just doesn't seem like an option when there are bills to pay. Is it better to get an entry-level job, even if it's not in your field, so that at least you can have some income while you look for better work?

Yes and no. According to an article in *The New York Times* on June 4, 2000, more and more young people are opting to spend their summers in low-paying or volunteer internships—instead of traditional summer jobs such as flipping burgers and lifeguarding—as preparation for the work world ahead. They've realized how competitive the work world has become in recent years and are starting early to prepare themselves for the career of their choice.

How do they do it and still manage to support themselves? Easy . . . as long as they have some money saved or can borrow from their parents for a while. But if you're paying your own way (and most of you reading this book will be), a nonsalaried internship—even if it's exactly what you've always wanted to do in the field of your choice—just doesn't seem possible.

It is. You'll just have to work a little harder and be a little more creative about your scheduling. Of course, if there *is* an entry-level paying job similar to the internship you're interested in, go for it. But if that job doesn't exist—or you're not quite qualified enough to land it—try these internship survival tactics.

- **Maximize your experience.** If you've got a limited time to work for free, maximize your experience by extending your hours to full time, or if that's not a possibility, work a few internships simultaneously. (Two is usually plenty.)

- **Ask for a stipend.** Some companies, especially if they want to keep you, might be able to offer you a small amount—enough, say, to cover your rent for a month. Supplement this with small loans from parents or friends, savings, or . . .

- **Get another job.** Intern/volunteer positions are usually very flexible about accommodating your paying gig. See if you can find part-time work in the evenings, every other day, or on weekends, giving you time to pursue your dream for ten to twenty hours a week. (Plenty for an internship.) You'll be a little brain-dead at the end, but the experience you'll have gotten will be more than worth it.

Buh-Bye

When everything's said and done—they've had the farewell party, told you that there will never be another intern like you, and enshrined your filing area as "Intern Alley"—it's time for you to return the favor. Write a polite thank-you letter and arrange a wrap-up meeting with your superior so that you can give each other feedback on the job and your performance. At this point, it's a good idea to get a recommendation, while your excellent character and hard work are still fresh in your employer's mind. Get a copy for yourself, or let your boss keep it on file for sending out as the need arises. Just don't lose track of him or her. Get your boss's card and stay in touch with a regular postcard now and again.

Have They Sweat?

"Summer work experience in our field counts an enormous amount. Lots of people are smart, but you have to have had the experience of sweat running down your brow, because a team project isn't finished and it isn't even your fault, but you're a part of this group and it has to get done tonight and it has to be perfect."

—Investment banker

Internship as Practice

Besides offering you a chance to get experience in your field—and rub elbows with folks who could help you in your career—getting an internship allows you to go through the same process that you'd go through for getting a real job. The confidence you've gained will only help as you head out on your search.

And the bottom line? Many companies, large and small, end up hiring former interns for full-time, permanent positions. Not bad for a couple of months of coffee-fetching and helping on projects, huh?

CHAPTER 9

Where Do I Find a Job?

Ten years of looking through the classifieds—a few of them in the early 1990s, the toughest job market in decades—have left this writer with a single sensory image of job hunting: that awful black-gray newsprint that gets all over your fingers and then lands on your refrigerator door, your light switches, and your face.

Is it so bleak, then? Is finding a job all red pens and smudges?

The answer, of course, is no. We are happy to report that the state of the job hunt is alive and well and rejuvenated by the entrance of a recent job-finding resource: yes, it's the Internet again. Type "employment" into AltaVista and no fewer than 7,991,305 sites come back, many with jobs searchable and sortable by type and income, most with e-mail addresses so you can zip your resume to the appropriate person. And, best of all, no newsprint!

Improved Avenues to Employment

Over the past decade or so, nothing short of a revolution in job-searching tools has taken place, and online listings have initiated the shake-up. What's even more remarkable is that rather than replacing traditional methods of job hunting (job placement centers, networking, classifieds, temp agencies, and the like), online classifieds have simply enriched what's already out there, making it even easier— and even a little bit fun—to locate a job.

With so much suddenly so accessible, this book will give you only a taste of what's out there for job seekers. Test the waters, and then plunge in. A few books may help you navigate the offerings. Try J. Michael Farr's *America's Top Jobs for College Graduates* (Jist Works, 1999) and *Jobs That Don't Suck* by Charlie

Drozdyk (Ballantine Books, 1998). Of course, there's always the online employment sites. The biggies—Monster.com, Jobs.com, HotJobs.com, and Careerbuilder.com—have hundreds of links to help you in all aspects of your search.

Your College's Career/Employment Center

How to Get Hired (Almost) Without Leaving Campus

As good as the Internet is, nothing beats a personal connection when you're trying to find a job. That's where your college's career/employment center comes in. Before you start slogging through the websites, remember that you have an incredible resource available to you just by picking up the telephone.

If you're still an undergrad, great. Your center is probably right around the corner (or at least only a bus ride away). Call them up and make an appointment to see a staff counselor. She'll familiarize you with everything your school's center has to offer, as well as set you up with a search plan tailored to your particular needs and schedule. Remember that it's never too early to start checking in. Centers usually offer everything from personality/vocational testing to information about summer internships and interviewing to mini-workshops in stress management. And that's not to mention hundreds (if not thousands) of job and company listings all around the world, many with a special fondness for hiring graduates of *your* school.

> ### Six Degrees of Separation
>
> **Deborah Novick** went to visit the job placement office at the University of Pennsylvania often during the year she was a senior. "I kept dropping my resume in the drop slots for different recruitment interviews," Deborah recalls. She was eventually selected to interview for Macy's. "At the interview, the guy was reading my resume, and he said, 'Echo Lake. You're an Echo Laker?' We had both worked as camp counselors at the same camp. Then he said, 'Novick . . . that sounds familiar.' And at the same time we both said 'Bob.' It turned out he had been my brother's camp counselor. He said, 'I'll make sure I get you to New York, but don't let me down.'"
>
> The second interviewer did not turn out to be from her kindergarten class or anything like that, but Deborah apparently did pretty well anyway, because she was hired immediately and has worked there ever since.

A couple thousand miles and a few years away from the old alma mater? Fret not. Most career centers are geared toward alumni as well as current students, and even if you can't get to campus, they may have a website (often with listings) and/or a counselor you can talk to over the phone.

Either way, your school's career center is the place to start. Why? Because they offer every conceivable resource a job hunter needs, from the beginning of the process (what do I want to do?) to the end (should I take this job or the other one?) and everything in between—*for free*. (Out in the real world it's called "career counseling" and it costs up to $200 an hour.) Still skeptical? Here's a rundown of what kinds of services a good career/employment center may offer.

- Personality and vocational testing (such as the Strong-Campbell Interest Inventory and the Meyers-Briggs Test)

- Resume-writing help and mock interviews

- Resource libraries with information about different fields' hiring practices and salary ranges; books on where to find jobs, internships, and work abroad; current professional periodicals; and company directories

- Mini-workshops in career-related topics

- Alumni contacts, mentor programs, and informational interviews

- Internship information

- Job listings

- Corporate recruiting

- Recommendation files for students

- Graduate school information and reference books

- Online resources and computer counseling

And the best service of all? An entire staff whose sole mission is to help you find a job that you like. In other words, people willing to help you explore your options and see what kind of career is best for you. Not bad, huh? (Eventually, they figure one of you will remember the help you got from your school's career center and pay them back by endowing a new dorm or something.)

To make sure that you're getting all the attention you deserve from those very same counselors, be aggressive—but *politely* so—during your hunt. That means don't just show up the last day of your senior year demanding a job. You've got to lay some groundwork to get noticed. Attend a few workshops, meet with counselors once or twice, spend a couple of weekday afternoons in the resource library. And of course, live up to your commitments once you've gotten the interviews (that means showing up prepared!) and thank the center staff when you eventually (and you will) land a job.

Connections and Networking

As in, "I got some *connections*. They'll take care a dis for ya" and "Can't make it to racquetball, Ted. Skip and I are meeting at the club for some G&Ts and some *networking*."

How is it that these two fairly ordinary words manage to sound both ominous and snooty at the same time? And why are they so important to finding a job?

In answer to the first question: Blame it on Hollywood. The truth is, all of us have connections, as well as our own network of relatives, friends, and associates; we just have to learn how to use them. And use them we should, especially when looking for a job. (You may not want to use your parents' money, but you certainly should use their connections!) After all, finding a job is a pretty personal affair. Despite what people say about keeping the professional and the personal separate, when it comes down to it, you're going to end up spending a lot of time at your job, and things you spend a lot of time doing have a way of becoming, well, *personal*. There's no getting around it. Your job says something about *you*—what you care about and how you've chosen to live.

Networking and connections are personal in the same way. Essentially, they help you widen the circle of people who want to help you do what you want to do. Think of it like this: A connection is someone who thinks well of you. Networking is just expanding the number of people who think the same thing. Simple, huh? Once you get your first job, you'll have begun building your very own network of folks to call for help on projects, career changes, or basic problem-solving when things get tough. In the meantime, use other people's networks: your family's, your friends', your university's. The list goes on.

A Persistent Lawyer

Allan Wolk went straight to law school after he graduated from college. However, after getting his law degree from Boston University, he realized that what he really wanted to do was to get into the creative end of advertising. "I put together a book," which is a portfolio of ads for real and made-up products, Allan explains, "with a lot of advice from a teacher. It took about six months. Four months after that I had my first job."

How did he go about looking? "In advertising, there's something called *The Red Book*—a lot of industries have something similar—that lists all the different advertising agencies and the names of the officers of the company. I would find somebody with a friendly sounding name, and I would call them. Of course, with any creative endeavor, everyone has his own opinion about what he likes and doesn't like, which can be pretty devastating when you're new and you don't know whom to trust. I made the decision to trust only my teacher.

"When somebody said they liked my work but didn't have any openings right now, I would ask them, 'Do you know of anybody else who's looking?' And that's how I eventually got my first job. Somebody sent me to somebody else, and that man sent me to a *third* person at Jordan McGrath, who wound up hiring me."

What keeps young'uns—that's you—from actually *using* their network of connections? Maybe they're shy. Maybe they think they're imposing on that alum/friend of the family/former boss. Listen carefully: *You're not imposing on anyone.* Believe it or not, people actually *enjoy* being asked for advice—it's flattering. And if you're shy, well, it's time to get over it. You've got to have at least a little bit of gumption to get out and find a job. Why not practice on someone who actually knows you? Even *likes* you? Anyway, the truth about connections is that while they get you in the door, the rest is up to you. Employers are looking for a good fit—whether you make a good impression depends on you and you alone.

Networking and connections function a lot more simply than you probably thought. First, do your homework. Find out about a prospective profession by looking in the usual places (online, in the library, and—*surprise!*—in your school's career center). Then pick up the phone and call some folks. It's that easy. Ask them about their jobs, how they got to where they are, what they like most (and least) about their chosen profession. Then sock it to 'em: "So how might a young person like me break into your field?" is one way to deepen the conversation. Or, "I read in last week's paper that newer workers in your industry have a high burnout rate. What advice would you have for someone who wants to make a long-term commitment?"

Follow up with a letter to your contact expressing your interest in their field and thanking them for their time. Try to mention something specific about your conversation that you found especially interesting, compelling, or insightful. Be sure to include all of your contact information, so they know how to contact you should they hear of any opportunities in the future for which you'd make a good match.

And with that, your not-quite-informational interview is now complete, and you've got the start of a beautiful network.

> ### An Investigator Does His Research
>
> **Josh Margulies** was looking through the job listings at the Columbia College job placement office, and came upon a listing that he decided must have gotten there by mistake: "It said, 'investigator for the investigative arm of the state legislature; power to subpoena, power to swear witnesses.' I looked at that and said to myself, 'They've got to be kidding.' I mean, I'm only twenty-one years old. I was the only Columbia grad who was crazy enough to even apply."
>
> The listing didn't say who was actually doing the hiring, but Josh went to the library, and found out everything he could about the state senator who chaired the committee. "I knew who the guy was, I knew the name of his dog . . . ."
>
> Josh also decided that a personal connection couldn't hurt. "It was really funny, but I found out that the senator who chairs the committee is the county chair for the party, and naturally, he knows all the county chairs from around the state. And I happened to have delivered newspapers for the former county chair from my hometown. So my mom called him, and he wrote me a great recommendation."
>
> When Josh got to the interview, it was the state senator himself who was doing the interviewing. "He asked me about my family, and I told him that my sister had graduated with honors from Harvard, *too*. He said, 'Oh, did you go to Harvard?' and I said, 'No, sir. You did.'" The rest, as they say, is history.

Employment/Temp Agencies, Career Counselors, and Headhunters

Of course, there may come a time when all those connections—and your burgeoning network—might not come through for you. Lucky you live in America! As with almost anything in this great demo-capitalist experiment, if there's a will—and a buck to be made—there's a way. Don't have a network of your own? There are several thousand employment agencies, career counselors, and headhunters out there willing to put you in touch with theirs. For a fee, of course.

Employment/Temp Agencies

What They Do

Basically, an employment agency contracts with employers to find competent workers in to fill various positions. For you (the employee), they take away a lot of the hassle of finding a job (no scanning the classifieds, one interview often suffices for many). For the employer, they take care of nasty things like taxes and Social Security payments, since you are actually an employee of the temp agency rather than the company you're working at, unless the employer buys out your contract. Employment/temp agencies also pre-screen you for basic skills and a hireable personality. The downside of all this is that the employment agency also takes away most of your bargaining power. You're not allowed to discuss salary with your employer, and any day-to-day grievances must go through the agency.

How They Work

Employment agencies are paid by the employer. You don't pay anything, but you should be at least vaguely aware of what they're adding on to your rate—about 15 to 25 percent for your basic office worker. Why should you care about the money they're making off you? Because it gives you a better idea of what companies will actually pay for someone to do your job. (It also explains why salary ranges at temp agencies can sometimes be a bit lower than what you'd get if you got the job yourself.)

> ### Would You Like to See My Other Piercings?
>
> "Every once in a while someone will come in looking appropriate, so we send her out for an interview the next day, and then the employer calls, and I'm saying to this guy, 'What do you mean, she was wearing an earring through her nose?'"
>
> —Randy Schaefer,
> employment agent,
> Rand Associates

What You Can Expect When You Show Up

You'll go through an interview and several kinds of tests, including knowledge of different computer applications, typing speed, spelling/grammar, and employee "values" such as, "Is it all right to take paper clips from the office to use at home?" (No.) "Should I talk about my salary with my employer?" (No.) "If I'm really frustrated, should I threaten my boss for higher wages?" (No, no, no.) Also, there will be a paperwork session where you will fill out your tax forms and citizenship documentation, for which you'll need your Social Security card and one other form of ID, and where they'll tell you about how their timecard payment system works.

What to Look For

Different types of agencies will specialize in different kinds of employment opportunities. National companies like Adecco and Manpower cover a range of office positions, from mailroom clerks to Web programmers to executive assistants. There's also Labor Ready, which specializes in manual labor jobs, and Artisan (in New York and Chicago) for creative jobs (copywriters, film editors, proofreaders, and the like). There are even a few employment agencies for independent school teachers. Carney Sandoe, based in Boston, places thousands of teaching candidates a year and is a good place to start if you're looking to get into the boarding-school racket. In terms of perks, some career counseling and software training is available from your basic no-frills employment agency, though many tend to be "move 'em in and move 'em out" kinds of places. Look for an agency where your "employment specialist" remembers your name and calls you often for jobs. This means that *you* have to keep in touch, too. Some top-notch employment/temp agencies offer health benefits once you've logged a certain number of hours and, as mentioned, software training, career counseling, networking cocktail parties, and a T-shirt around the holidays.

Reasons to Temp Rather Than Take a Full-Time Job Right Away

1) Doing well at a temp job shows the agency you deserve a shot at their best full-time listings.

2) You'll earn enough money to survive while you're looking for something in the—pardon the expression—field of your dreams.

3) If they like you, the company you're working at may offer you a full-time job. (Be aware that they'll also be paying a fee to buy your contract with the temp agency. Also, only go full-time if it truly meshes with your future plans.)

4) No aspirations? Temping lets you try out several different types of jobs in many kinds of companies.

On the Job

Most agencies deal in glorified secretary work, but they'll assure you that these are promotable positions, which is usually true. If you're a star, your abilities will be recognized no matter where you start out, even if it's in the telemarketing booth. Remember, though, that it's difficult to show passion if you're in a job you don't like. Though an employment agency prizes, above all, a "flexible" worker, don't sell yourself short. You need to know when "flexible" is code for push-aroundable.

How to Get an Employment Agency to Give You Its All

An employment agency, like any boss, will be impressed by someone who's done his homework. Present yourself in this way and they are more likely to find you a job. Arrive on time and well dressed, with a notebook, a plan, and a positive attitude. Once you've found an agency you like, stick with them—they'll repay you in higher wages and better assignments. Don't, however, feel the need to limit yourself to just one agency. Play the field. Just be sure you know your favorites.

How to Find One

The best way to find one you like is through a referral. They'll like you because you're so-and-so's equally brilliant and dependable friend, and your friend will like you because she'll probably get a little kickback from the referral. Visit and see if you like the place. Is the staff welcoming? Stuffy? Patronizing? Perfect? What resources do they offer job seekers (computer lab, resume workshops, etc.)? A dingy little office will tell you a lot about what kind of "Fortune 5,000" clients Number One Temps *really* has. Finally, ask them who's paying the fee for the placement. Bottom line: It should not be you.

Career Counselors

What They Do

The best career counselors will be able to give you—for $50 to $200 an hour—most of the services your college career center gave you for *free*. Just like at school, job counseling, vocational testing, resume doctoring, practice interviewing, and job listings are all available, but this time for a price.

What to Look For

Again, get a recommendation from someone. Contact your town's Better Business Bureau to check whether yours is a reputable counselor. Never sign on with a private counselor until you meet him or her, and don't sign up for a package deal; you should be able to pay as you go. It's important to remember that a career counselor can't do everything. You still have to create the resume, go to the interview, and get the job. Which begs the question: Why pay for something you're just going to have to end up doing yourself anyway?

Cheaper Ways to Get Career Counseling

Check out career workshops run by community colleges, libraries, and other civic institutions; career counseling online through one of the major job-finding sites (see the Online Job Search section on page 107); your school's career/employment center; career-planning books and websites; and advice from friends and family.

Headhunters

What They Do

Otherwise called "executive recruitment firms," headhunters specialize in filling high-level corporate positions.

How They Work

Basically, there are two kinds of recruiting firms. The first is a retainer firm, hired by a corporation to find someone they need. These folks are looking for experienced talent, usually in the $100,000-and-up range. If this is you, you probably don't need to be reading this chapter. In other words, don't be expecting a call from a retainer firm anytime soon. The other kind of headhunter is called a contingency firm. They get paid only when their work results in a hire. Although these companies, too, are primarily looking for experienced workers, they may be more likely than a retainer firm to take a chance on a new college grad. In any case, both are recommended only if you have a very clear idea of what kind of work you want in which field—not for the merely inquisitive.

Classified Ads

While networking and your college placement center are still your best bets for future employment, just because you're connected doesn't mean you should dis the help wanted ads. Advertiser of stinker jobs and hidden gems both, facilitator of yucky newsprint to all clean surfaces of the earth, the classifieds are the foundation of any serious job search, and you'll be well advised to pay attention to them.

Basically, classifieds are found in four separate kinds of publications: national, local, professional trade, and online. To get the most out of these listings, you'll need to look in the appropriate places. If you want to be a stock analyst, the *Sacramento Bee* may not be the best place to look. *The Wall Street Journal* or *The New York Times* would more likely carry what you're looking for jobwise. This means knowing which publications list jobs particular to your field. *The New York Times'* "Week in Review" as well as the *Higher Education Supplement* list educational positions in secondary schools and colleges; *Ad Age* carries jobs in advertising; and MediaBistro.com contains jobs in publishing. Read *Variety* for audition notices on stage and in film and television.

Though it's always a good idea to hone your search to just a few relevant sections of the classifieds (e.g., bypassing "Acctg." and "Waitstaff" if you're a software designer), realize that ads are usually listed alphabetically and can turn up in the weirdest places. Avoid the want ads placed by employment agencies, though, as well as jobs that offer EXCITING CAREER OPPTY!!! $60K TO START!!! WORK FROM YOUR HOME!!! While there are a few free lunches in this world, they don't usually get advertised in the newspaper.

Moreover, don't limit your browsing to entry-level or junior positions. If there is a senior position advertised, it might mean shake-up in that department. Send your resume as a query—you never know what might turn up.

The Great Ego-Stroke

Andrea Poe got her first job through a *New York Times* want ad. Andrea had just finished college and knew that she wanted to be in design, but she wasn't sure how to get started. "I saw this ad in the *Times*," Andrea says. "It said 'Personal assistant to designer.' I applied, and I couldn't believe it when it turned out to be Oleg Cassini! I have no idea why he bothered to advertise, but I'm glad he did." She went through four separate interviews before she landed the job. "After the first interview, of course, I ran out and found his autobiography, *In My Own Fashion*, and read the whole thing in time for the second interview. I kind of liked it, and I think he could tell."

A guide to the classifieds:

- **National classifieds:** Internet classified sites have mostly taken the place of the old traditional-media national classifieds, but there are two services you may want to keep in mind if you're looking for a job nationwide. *National Ad Search* (800-992-2832) is a weekly compendium of classifieds from all around the country. Also, the *National Business Employment Weekly*, issued by *The Wall Street Journal*, gives all the help-wanted ads listed in their regional editions. The drawback to national classifieds? You're hampered a little by time, as the jobs listed tend to be reprints of those that have already appeared in earlier editions of the paper. An online nationwide job search may be a better bet.

- **Local classifieds:** The more geographically specific, the better, according to many career counselors. Why? Smaller companies almost always list open jobs in the local paper. These are the kinds of jobs that are perfect for first-time job seekers, as a smaller company may be more likely to take a chance on someone less experienced. Plus, there's more room to grow in the company and, because there's probably less bureaucracy, greater opportunities for advancement.

A Question of Semantics

Andrea Paykin was in no particular hurry to find a job after college. Her parents, she explains, understood completely: "'Take your time,' they told me." Several months later, they told her to leave and not to come back until she'd found a job. "It was very unlike them," Andrea says, loyally. She went through the help-wanted ads and saw one that seemed interesting, working as an editorial assistant at Daniel Weiss Associates, a publisher that puts out romance novels. The advertisement said, "resumes only—no calls."

Andrea figured that going to see them in person wasn't really a call, so she turned up at their offices and talked her way in to see the guy who was going to make the hire. "He had a huge pile of resumes on his desk. He looked at the resumes, looked at me, and said, 'I can't deal with all these resumes,' and hired me."

- **Professional trade classifieds:** These can be be found in indices like the *Gale Directory of Publications and Broadcast Media*, the *Encyclopedia of Associations* (both from Gale Research, Inc., Detroit), or the *Standard Periodical Directory* (Oxbridge Communications). Professional trade classifieds are geared toward professionals, so there are fewer entry-level positions advertised. However, you can use them to get a sense of which companies are hiring and firing, and which industries are on their way up— hiring lots of young people—or down.

- **Internet classifieds:** Up-to-the-minute listings that are searchable, sortable, and easily printed out? And you can respond immediately by e-mailing a resume and a cover letter? It's hard to beat the online classifieds. Check Careerbuilder.com for newspaper classifieds from around the country online and sites like Monster.com, Jobs.com, and HotJobs.com for Internet-only listings. To really jump into your online job search using the Internet's networking capabilities for all their worth, read on!

Online Job Search

Chances are, you're already plenty savvy about the *huge* opportunities for finding jobs online. You are a charter member of the "digital generation," after all. Behind the million-dollar television ads for career sites, however, it's important that we realize that the Internet has basically just improved and expanded on (about a gazillionfold) the same old networking concept we were talking about at the beginning of this chapter. Listings are no longer limited only to those in town. The Internet has made it possible for us to look all around the *world* for jobs, to apply instantly via e-mail, and to get in contact with employers through resume postings, individual websites, and electronic portfolios.

Guiding Your Online Job Search

There are quite a few books to help you get the most out of your Internet search, but we recommend Pat Kendall's *Jump Start Your Online Job Search in a Weekend* (Prima Publishing, 2000) and *110 Best Job Search Sites on the Internet* by Katherine K. Yonge (Linx Education Pub. Inc., 1998). If you'd rather go all-electronic, most of the major sites have pages devoted to guiding and refining your search techniques. Or you can focus your search through your favorite service, typing in "employment" or "jobs" to get you started.

Employment Sites

These include online listings of newspaper classifieds as well as job listings available *only* on the Internet.

- **General employment:** Careerbuilder.com, Monster.com, Jobs.com, HotJobs.com

- **Advertising/Marketing/PR:** Mediabistro.com, HireMinds.com

- **Business/Financial:** Jobsinthemoney.com

- **Education:** Teachers.net

- **Engineering:** Engineeringjobs.com

- **Entertainment/Broadcasting:** Entertainment-jobs.net

- **Freelance/project work:** eLance.com, Guru.com

- **Journalism/Writing:** NewsJobs.net, JournalismJobs.com, FreelanceWriting.com

- **Law/Government:** LawJobs.com

- **Medical:** md-jobs.com, Medicaljobsonline.com

- **Publishing/Design/Media:** Mediabistro.com, Guru.com, HireMinds.com

- **Not-for-profit/Social services/Environmental:** Nonprofit.com, OpportunityNOCs.org, Environmental-jobs.com

- **Tech/Dot-com:** HireMinds.com, Techies.com

Let's Go Surfin' Now

Besides giving you the chance to pore through the listings, the Internet is an excellent place to get a sense of a given field or company in which you're interested. Most companies will have some kind of website that gives information about the company, its culture, and its employees. Even better, they'll also usually have a human resources page where they list recent job openings and contact information on where to send your resume.

Listserv Forums, Chat, and Discussion Groups

These provide another good place to find information about employment. Don't be shy about posting a query such as, "My name is Jane Doe and I'm looking to get into the field of documentary filmmaking. Any advice on how to break in?" There are thousands of people all around the world who, for some reason, actually *enjoy* responding to discussion group queries, and you'll be surprised how many people will be willing to help you. As with all online meetings, don't give out any personal information until you've checked to make sure your e-mail pal is legit.

Digital Resumes, Portfolios, Etc.

Some employment sites have a place where you can post your resume for employers to see. If you'd like to take your job search a step beyond this, however, or if you're an artist or writer who'd like to have a place where folks can see your work instantly, consider creating your own self-promoting website. (For more on this, see chapter 13.) For casual queries, this is a great way to give an employer a sense of who you are at a glance. Include your resume, contact information, and examples of what you do (writing clips, artwork, design, teaching portfolio, etc.).

CHAPTER 10

How Do I Get the Job?

After everything's said and done, and you've pulled every string you could, used every connection you've got, combed the classifieds for the choicest job listings you could find, and dazzled them with your digital portfolio, you've still got just three basic ways to convince any given company that you've got what it takes to do the job: your resume, your cover letter, and an interview. Making the most out of these fundamentals is what this chapter is all about.

First, you've got to know a little bit about what Mr. and Ms. Employer want. How are you going to wow 'em with your dazzling resume/cover letter/interview combination unless you have at least a rough picture of what they're looking for? (Don't worry—filling the bill will be much easier than you'd expect.)

Before He Was No. 23

Mike Jordan spent his first three years of college at the London School of Economics. He spent his senior year at Drew University, keeping up a full course load while working four days a week selling insurance for the Equitable. "My boss at the Equitable was fired," Mike says. "They offered me a full-time job, but the salary was lower than what I'd been making while I was still in college."

He put 150 resumes in a briefcase and went to New York City. "It was just an instinct. I went to the financial district and midtown, and went into office buildings that looked likely, picked names from the directories, took the elevator upstairs, and just walked in." He dropped off over a hundred resumes. "I went in like a salesman: 'Hi, my name is Mike Jordan.'" One of the companies he visited was Showtime, the cable television network. They called him in for an interview and hired him to work in their accounting department.

What Employers Want

- **Youth:** Although you might not believe it, you've already got some things employers greatly value in a new hire: optimism, a willingness to work for relatively little money, and a desire to excel. If you're a recent college graduate, you're being hired not so much for your skills as for your promise. And you didn't even have to do anything for it.

- **Passion:** Also known as ambition, excitement, curiosity, or "fire in the belly," passion is what makes you do the best job you can, pull long hours where someone a little more jaded may have punched out at five, and even (and this is what makes you *really* popular with employers) do a job for little or no money just because you want to get your foot in the door.

- **The perfect worker:** Whatever *that* means. In truth, the definition of the ideal candidate is more elastic than you would think. "Highly ambitious perfectionist with an eagle eye for details" works for some employers, while "flexible, down-to-earth people person with a good personality" works for others. It depends on the job and the whim of your boss. Come to think of it, it's kind of like a relationship. You're *you,* so find a good match for the person you are, not some predetermined idea of what makes a good employee. (Although if *who you are* is consistently late, unreliable, and prone to office theft, you may not be quite what they're looking for.)

- **Experience:** Finding some way to get experience in your career area *before* you finish college is always a good idea. It tells employers that you're interested and indicates your passion for your field. Remember, though, that experience doesn't have to mean a two-year, full-time job doing exactly the job for which you're applying. A few internships, some creative extracurricular work, and even special course work related to your field can show an employer you're committed. See chapter 8 for more information on how to get experience, as well as the section on resumes in this chapter for how to make the most of it on paper.

- **Good grades:** While an excellent academic record will impress most employers, a couple of tarnishes here and there won't necessarily disqualify you from your dream job. Says an investment banker, "Grades signify the desire to achieve." True, but they don't necessarily measure intelligence or work-savvy, nor are they a particularly precise indicator of future business success.

Impress them with what you *have* succeeded in, and your D+ in freshman calculus recedes into the distant past, where it belongs.

- **A great attitude:** Entry-level work is not always fun and glamorous, and employers should not feel like they're groveling to get you to do the "Two Fs and a P" (faxing, filing, and photocopying). It's called paying your dues, and we've all done it.

- **People skills:** This includes the ability to play along with and motivate your coworkers, grace under pressure, and a knack for handling group dynamics—basically, being "a team player." Sound like your own personal vision of hell? Perhaps you might consider the time-honored profession of hermit/mystic mountain dweller. That, or become a writer. (Come to think of it, even writers have to deal with other people once in a while. You've got to get material.) Get the point? You may want to develop your people skills after all.

They Don't Consider It Pestering

Nicole Poses began her job search with a visit to the job placement center at her college. She was in her senior year at Syracuse and knew she wanted to get into marketing—specifically, at a cosmetics firm. She was going through the list of companies that would be recruiting at Syracuse that spring when she saw a listing for Estée Lauder; unfortunately, the listing said they were looking only for engineers.

"I made friends with the head recruiter in New York, called him every day, and annoyed him until he agreed to give me an interview," Nicole says. "I didn't think I'd get a second interview since I wasn't an engineer, but they called me a couple of weeks later and flew me down to New York City to interview for a marketing job. I thought it went horribly, and I cried when I left, because I really wanted the job and I was sure I didn't get it—and then I got it."

- **A perfectionist:** That is, an easygoing perfectionist, as opposed to the obsessive-compulsive/sharpen all your pencils so they're the exact same height/send e-mails about "certain messy food containers in the office kitchen" kind.

- **Steady performance:** In college you may have been able to skip a few days, even flunk a test, and in the end, even it all out by aceing your final exam. Not so in the real world. You've actually got to show up every day, dressed appropriately (walk-of-shame outfits are definitely discouraged), smelling nothing like day-old beer and cigarettes. Reliability isn't just prized; it's required. In some cases, you've also got to make small talk with the folks at the coffeepot. In others, you actually have to be able to *think*. In other words, at work—as opposed to school—there is a basic level of competency below which you cannot fall. It has to do with the whole salary thing. In college, you paid the bills; at work, someone's paying you. Big difference.

In the end, employers just want you to work hard, acquire skills and be well rounded and easy to work with on a regular basis. Of course, they also want your passion and your vision, and it would be nice if you were tremendously interested in the field you want to enter—enough to do your homework and inform yourself about it. Oh, and good hygiene, and no criminal record, and a good sense of humor. And they want this all right from the get-go—neatly packaged and succinctly expressed in a cover letter, a resume, and a half-hour interview.

But you *are* all those things! The question is, how do you get them to see that in, say, two pieces of paper and questions like, "What, in your opinion, is your greatest weakness?" and "So, tell me about that D+ in calculus."

The Great Resume

This is where the proverbial buck starts and stops. Besides being the foundation upon which you can build a great cover letter and a great interview, a great resume (or CV in some circles, short for curriculum vitae) is your single most effective tool for marketing the priceless masterpiece that is *you*. And while this chapter will give you a heads-up on how to go about getting your resume (and cover letter and interview techniques) into shape, you'd be wise to delve further into the subject by taking a look at the following books: *The Complete Resume & Job Search for College Students* by Robert Lang Adams, Laura Morin, and Bob Adams (Adams Media, 1999) and *Trashproof Resumes: Your Guide to Cracking the Job Market* by Timothy D. Haft (The Princeton Review, 1995). You can also look for resume samples on the Web, at sites like JobWeb.org and WritingResumes.com. They'll give you a good idea of what people are including and how they're presenting that information. For highly specialized careers—tech jobs, higher-level scientific jobs, academic postings—or positions where image is everything, like graphic design, what your resume says and how it looks can make or break an opportunity (more about this in chapter 13).

Be forewarned: If you don't already have one, creating a resume can be something of an emotional experience. Maybe it has something to do with trying to fit your whole educational and professional life into a single page. You end up feeling, well, a lot less *accomplished* than you'd like. The good news is that this feeling changes as you get older, and you actually start to be a little proud of your resume. In the meantime, you've got to start somewhere.

A Resume's Appearance

First of all, there should *not be any typos*. Employers use stupid little mistakes like these as a way to reduce the number of applicants. No matter how good your resume, you'll look careless and rushed (read: undesirable) if you have spelling or grammatical errors on your resume. Your resume should be typed and printed with a high-resolution printer on plain high-quality white paper. The font on your resume should, ideally, match your cover letter. What's more, the font should be easy to read and 12-point or larger, without too many fancy italics or curlicues. (Just because you can read it with your twentysomething pair of eyes doesn't mean everyone else will.) Design is crucial; it should have clean lines and fit on a single page.

Structure of a Resume

A basic business resume is composed of three main sections: education, work experience, and activities. There are several others you may want to add as well, depending on your experience: skills (especially computer knowledge), languages, travel, community work (for nonprofit/social services), personal background, publication history, and references. How the sections should be ordered will vary from person to person, depending on how long you've been out of school and what you're trying to accomplish. Most likely if you're a recent graduate, the education section will be first.

- **Education:** Schools should be listed in reverse chronological order, starting with the school most recently attended and working backward. Include college name, location, dates of attendance, date you received your degree, what type of degree, major, GPA (if above 3.2), honors (cum laude, etc.), and awards. You can also have a separate "Honors and Awards" section. Include any educational experience or course work that fits with the job or industry to which you're applying. This includes your senior thesis—if it's related, describe it briefly. Include your high school only if it's a prestigious prep school that may be recognized by a potential employer or if you attended a special high school for a trade or art and you're pursuing a career in that area.

- **Work experience:** Again, reverse chronological order. Include all the work you're proud of, paid or unpaid, even if the experience was relatively brief. Include job title, organization you worked for, location, and dates. Put these in any order that sounds most impressive. For example, instead of "Current Events, San Diego, CA, assistant to the public relations director, summer of 1998," try "Public Relations Assistant, Current Events, San Diego, CA, summer of 1998." Use the active voice, as in, "Wrote and designed

> ### Lifeguarding Doesn't Count
>
> "The most important thing on a resume is quality internships, or substantial work during the summer. People come in to us, and they can type fifty words a minute, but they have no idea how to write a business letter."
>
> —Kathy Klein,
> employment agent,
> Career Blazers

Currents, the agency's weekly in-house newsletter." Also, try to include moments that stand out in your work experience. Not frivolous ones, but things that may make your resume unique and memorable.

Completed projects work well here—for example, say during your fictional job at Current Events you created a new filing system for the agency's art files. Instead of "Created new filing system, organized old ads," why not write, "Revamped Current Events' art files, organizing traffic and production methods for storing, maintaining, and accessing past print production." Wow! All that and you fetch coffee, too? The more specific you are in your descriptions—showing that you actually accomplished something tangible in your work—the stronger your resume.

- **Activities:** Depending on the length of this section and your personal experiences, you can break it down to more specific headings, such as "Overseas Travel" (great for jobs that are looking for bilingual applicants or people with overseas experience); "Community Work" (essential if you're looking for a job in the not-for-profit sector or the "helping professions," like social work, community organizing, and education); or professional accomplishments, like "Performances," "Publication History," "Athletics," etc. The point of listing your activities is twofold. First, you want to convince your employer that you're not a school-to-work robot without any other interests. At the same time, you're trying to convince whomever is seeing your resume that even your extracurricular work fits in to what you'd like to do with your career.

- **Skills, languages, personal information:** In France, personal information (date of birth, marriage status, number of children) is required, as is a handwritten cover letter so they can check your penmanship. Fortunately, Americans are a little more concerned with privacy, and in the last sections of your resume, you should include only what you think will make you stand out as a better candidate. Computer skills, if you have them, should *definitely* be part of your resume. In addition to highlighting any specialized programs or languages you know (Quark, Java, HTML, etc.), don't be afraid to include your knowledge of some of the more ubiquitous software, too, like Microsoft Word and Excel, which will just set your prospective employers at ease that, yes, you do know how to use a mouse. Languages should be included *only* if you are fluent.

- **References:** Unless an employer asks that your references be included along with your resume and cover letter, "References available upon request" will suffice. This, however, means that you actually have the names and contact information (work phone number, address, and title) of three professional references—people who can vouch for both your performance and your personality—available when someone asks. "Professional" doesn't necessarily mean a former boss, though as you progress through the work world, this will be the case more and more often. A former professor's or mentor's reference will probably be what you use when you're just starting out and, if you stay in academic circles, for much longer. Some colleges even keep recommendations for alums in a central file, sending them out per your request. As mentioned in chapter 8, it's a good idea to get your recommendations while you're still fresh in the mind of that favorite boss/professor.

- **Career objective:** While some resumes include a sentence or two about your "career objective" (e.g., "Seeking an entry-level position in a fast-paced marketing organization"), most of these, as you can see by the example, sound canned and aren't really necessary unless you've got a really specific

> ### Don't Foul Up Your Resume
> Robert Half, head of Accountemps, counsels clients on their resumes. Here are excerpts from some first drafts presented to him over the years:
>
> **Grilled free-range deductions:**
> "Duties: Senior accountant, prepared journal entrees for companies."
>
> **And his memory is real good, too:**
> "Excellent memory; strong math aptitude; excellent memory; effective management skills; and very good at math."
>
> **But you can't make her think:**
> "My experience in horticulture is well-rooted."
>
> (Source: Accountemps)

job in mind. We suggest making an expanded, focused version of your career objective part of your cover letter.

Customizing Your Resume

Bottom line: You can't make anything up, and there are certain things, like your educational background and your major work history, that simply have to be included. But depending on the kind of position you're applying for, the type of company you'd be working in, and the way you'd like to appear on paper, you can make quite a few subtle adjustments to your resume to market yourself differently to different "customers." Employers expect you to represent your experience in the best light possible—heck, they probably did the same thing to get where they are—but they also expect truthfulness. Under each item describe in brief your accomplishments and duties in the position. Check out sample resumes from the different fields you're interested in (again, check out The Princeton Review's *Trashproof Resumes*), see what kind of skills are being highlighted for which fields, and create different versions of your own resume that cater to each. Take heed, however, every time you change your resume—even just the tiniest bit—and make sure you proofread the thing at least *twice* before you send it out again.

The Great Letter

A lot of people blow off their cover letters, preferring to send the same bland photocopied "Dear Human Resources Manager . . ." missive to all twenty-seven prospective employers just because it's less of a hassle. While individually tailored cover letters do take a bit more time, that's what earns them the title "great." Learning how to craft an excellent, personalized cover letter is well worth the effort. Not only will the skill last you for the rest of your career, but it will also get you noticed faster than the fanciest paper, the nicest fonts, and the most padded resume. Why? Because employers actually *do* take the time to at least glance over the cover letters they receive. If yours is honest, concise, specific, and conveys your personality, experience, and passion (and maybe a touch of humor thrown in for good measure), they may even like the thing. This alone sets you apart from, say, 90 percent of the other folks who are applying for the job.

What makes a great letter? First, the basics. The letter should be in business format (left justified, space between paragraphs, and single spaced), with no typos or spelling or grammatical errors. It shouldn't seem mass produced, and it should manage to convey in one page (1) the position for which you're applying, (2) why you think you'd be perfect for the job, (3) your relevant work/educational history, and (4) your current job/life situation and where you can be reached. If you're into being proactive, you can also include a line in the last paragraph letting them know that you'll be following up on your letter soon. For example: "I look forward to learning more about the position, and I'll be getting in touch soon." This is simply a courtesy. Usually, if an employer wants to talk to you, they'll call you; however, it doesn't hurt to let them know you'll be in touch. That way, when you do call, you can refer to your letter. This helps soften the introductions and gives you something of an "in."

> ### Thesaurus Time
> "If I see the word 'liaison' one more time, I'm going to throw up."
>
> —Human resources administrator

Remember what we said earlier about customization? Career counselors advise that your letter should be short and to the point—the point being that you have the qualifications for the job. At the same time, it should be as specifically geared as possible to what you know about the company and the field to which you're applying. Fortunately, if you're engaging in a wide search—even if it's across a few different industries—you can do all of this *and* keep the basic structure and content of your cover letter the same. All you need to do is change the pertinent details, refocusing key sentences and adding relevant experiences as necessary.

For example, let's look at the opening paragraph of Melissa Palacio's cover letter to a nationwide service organization.

> I'm seeking a position where I can connect my substantial experience working with young people with my interest in international travel and cross-cultural learning. As such, I'm writing to submit my resume for your recently advertised Diversity Recruitment Assistant Coordinator position.

She's identified the position for which she's applying, as well as her specific goals and reasons for applying. A great start. Now take a look at the same paragraph customized for a public television station in New York City. It offers the same basic structure and content (with two sentences added about public television), expressed differently.

> I'm seeking a position where I can connect my substantial experience working with young people with my interest in public television. I believe it's important that young people are not only the consumers, but also the creators, of culture. Public television has the potential to help young people cultivate their voice and share that voice with their communities, and I'd like to be a part of this effort. As such, I'm writing to submit my resume for your recently advertised Youth Outreach Junior Coordinator position.

Think it can't be done again? Read 'em and weep. Here's her opening paragraph for another educational/program coordinator position, this time for a public botanical garden.

> I'm seeking a position where I can connect my substantial experience working with young people with my interest in supporting urban green spaces. I believe it's important that young people have opportunities for hands-on learning about the natural environment. As such, I'm writing to submit my resume for your recently advertised Assistant Director of Children and Family Programs position.

The point of these examples is not to say that you should mass-produce your cover letters and send them out indiscriminately to a hundred different positions in thirty disparate fields. Quite the opposite. The position that Melissa was applying to in each case was remarkably similar—essentially an assistant educational outreach coordinator—and something for which she was well prepared by her work experience as a teacher and community organizer. Creating a good cover letter template like Melissa's meant allowing for customization and additions where necessary without having to reinvent the wheel each time.

There will be times, however, when this strategy just doesn't work—for example, when the employer requires certain specific information to be included, or when the job is so different from other types of positions you're applying for that it needs a whole new tone, content, or structure. In those instances you'll just have to write a wholly unique letter. It may be that you want a certain job so much that a standard letter just won't cut it, anyway. When such positions come up, you'll want to compose something new, fresh, and appropriately passionate. By all means, do. Your good old standby letter will be there waiting for you when you get back.

The Great Interview

Whether an interview is great or not pretty much depends on two things: you and the other person (or people, if it's a group meeting). And believe it or not, that's the whole point of an interview: to determine whether there's a good fit between you and the company for which you want to work. Once you've gotten past the resume and cover letter screening stages (both clearly good enough to get you in the door), the interview should really be about getting to know each other—seeing if there's a match between your skills and the company's needs, your interests and the company's opportunities.

Ummm . . . Well, It's Like . . . Know What I Mean?

"I don't have any particular questions that I ask. The point is not so much the question, or even their answer to the question, as how they can answer it. Can they speak in complete sentences? If they can, then they can probably write in complete sentences as well."

—Lawyer

They ask you questions *and you ask them questions*. Believe it or not, that's the secret to making an interview great: actually knowing something about the position you're interviewing for, and caring enough to ask questions pertinent to that position. Beyond any questions about your personality, your personal strengths and weaknesses, and your typing speed, it's the match that matters most, and when it's there, both of you will feel it.

Preparing Yourself

While it's important to find out as much as you can about the individual companies you'll be talking with—what they do, whether they've been in the news lately, their goals and mission—getting a general sense of their industry is probably where you'll focus most of your energy.

A genuine interest in the field will be the source of most of your good questions—not because you want to impress your interviewer, but because you actually want to know the answers. Also, it's not a bad idea to find out a little bit about the person who'll be interviewing you, if you know his or her name. Reach out to your network to see if anyone knows a bit about his or her work background. How long has she been with the firm? What are some of his accomplishments?

Preparing yourself also means coming up with a few responses to some of interviewing's Tried and True Questions. No matter who's doing the asking, there's usually going to be some *version* of the top ten, in order of frequency.

1.   Tell me about yourself.

2.   What do you see yourself doing five years from now?

3.   What is the accomplishment of which you are most proud?

4.   What do you know about this company?

5.   Why do you want to work here?

6.   What is your greatest weakness?

7.   Describe a difficult situation in your life and how you handled it.

8.   Tell me about your last job.

9.   Tell me about your college experience.

10.   What do you like to read?

They'll come in many different forms, but you'll recognize them instantly as "interview questions," and you'll want to have at least the skeleton of an answer ready. The best answers are not those that sound rehearsed ("I am a hard-working, detail-oriented team player with a lot of enthusiasm for fill-in-the-blank company, Sir!") or those that sound disingenuous ("My greatest weakness? Well, Marge, I'd have to say it's my commitment to perfection and obsession with working long hours"). Rather, they're the ones that actually say something about you and your real interests, your real goals, and your actual setbacks.

This last one is crucial. Companies like to ask questions about the harder times as well as the glory days. This isn't because of some innate sadistic impulse on their part, but because the real working world can throw you a curveball once in a while, and employers would like to know how you'd respond. Relating an in-

> **Think**
>
> "I'll ask them if they watch the show, and if they do I'll ask, 'What would you change to make it better?' I'm looking for a point of view. I don't want them just to say, 'It's great. There's nothing to change.' And I hope they're smart enough not to lie, because I'll know immediately."
>
> —Television producer

cident whereby you actually did overcome a challenge—and learned from it as a result—speaks for your ability to persevere and change. "Challenges" can be anything from a gap in your employment record to a bad grade in college to a difficult coworker. Keep it professional, however; truly personal challenges like your parents' divorce or your excessive alcohol consumption in college do not belong in the interview room.

Believe it or not, it takes a bit of practice to sound both confident *and* real—even if it's your twentieth telling of why you left your last job—so bounce ideas off your friends and family. Even better, take the opportunity to run through a mock interview at your college's job placement center to get a sense of what you sound like and how you're coming across. The idea is to have a few well-thought-out answers (and questions) in mind. Then, as with the cover letters, customize your responses according to the tone and direction of each individual interview.

Last-Minute Tips

When the day of reckoning finally arrives—you've done your research, prepared a few intelligent responses to some basic questions, and have a list (written down, in case you blank) of some questions you'd like to ask them—there are a few things you can do to cut down on the willies and increase your chances of the interview being a success.

Appearance Checklist

✓ Hair washed and combed

✓ No bad smells emanating from any where on body

✓ No overpowering good smells emanat-ing from anywhere on body

✓ Suit or nice dress freshly ironed

✓ Shoes shined

✓ Matching socks (men and women)

✓ Matching earrings (women only)

✓ A minimum of makeup (men and women)

- **Take care of yourself.** Eat a normal breakfast/lunch before your meeting. Don't drink too much coffee, and if you're a smoker, wait until after the interview. Trust me, you do not want to smell like stale cigarettes and coffee; anyway, they'll just make you jittery.

- **Look sharp.** Dress ap propriately for the kind of environment you'd be working in if you got the job. Basically, you should make your appearance a nonissue. This is especially important for companies where professional attire is required five days a week—"casual Friday" khakis and a sport blazer just won't cut it here.

- **Get there early.** The easiest way to ruin your chances of getting the job is to be late. Arrange your schedule and transportation so that you arrive ten minutes early. It will give you a chance to relax and go over your notes and questions before the interview.

- **Bring a few copies of your resume.** Most likely they'll have one in front of them, but carry some along with you just in case.

- **Get into it.** During the interview, it's important to be as focused and engaged as possible. Maintain eye contact, don't fidget or slouch, and if you're really nervous, try to slow down your speech and breathe. When you're responding to questions, try not to generalize. Think of each question as a mini-essay and respond as honestly and eloquently as possible.

- **Thank them.** Remember to thank your interviewer both during the interview and after. Write down the names of the people with whom you interviewed, and when you're home, send them a thank-you note. Be specific about what you discussed in the interview, finding a way to tie in your interest in the job. For example, in Melissa Palacio's interview with the botanical garden, she might have written, "I enjoyed talking with you about ways the botanical garden can increase community participation in educational events, and I'd just like to once more express my desire to be part of that effort."

After everything's said and done, remember that it's just you you're selling, and if you like and respect yourself, you'll do a good job at it. Gestures like asking good questions and thank-you letters shouldn't be phony attempts to ingratiate yourself to an employer. Rather, they're opportunities to tell them how much you actually enjoyed the interview and how much you'd like the job. Consider them as such and you've got a pretty good chance of actually landing it.

CHAPTER 11

I Got the Job—Now What?

You got it! That wasn't *too* hard, was it?

Hold off on the whoops of joy until after you've hung up the telephone—unless, of course, this is *it*, the one job you've been dying to get your whole life and would take even if they paid you in Monopoly money. If you're angling for a few jobs, on the other hand, or just not absolutely sure you want this one, make sure you understand the terms of the offer (start date, salary, benefits, and work schedule), politely and warmly thank the person who's doing the offering, and say that you'd like a day or two to finalize your decision. Make an appointment to get back to them at a certain time, and hang up the phone. Whoop all you want, then take a deep breath. You've got some thinking to do.

Why Wait?

Three reasons: time, choice, and money. As for the first, you may want some time to reflect back on your interview and what you learned about the company during the time you spent there. Did those corporate inspirational posters all over the place (PERSEVERANCE . . . TEAMWORK . . . COMPETITION . . . PROFIT) give you the creeps? Did your interviewer's comment about secretly hating his boss seem a little, well, odd? Or maybe you loved the company but in recalling your interview remembered a few issues you'd like to clarify before accepting the position. In any case, taking a few days to get your head together after the initial excitement can't hurt, and a good employer will respect your decision to wait a bit.

The second reason has to do with choice. If you're like most, it's likely that you applied for more than one job during your search, and waiting a few days to see which offers come through isn't rude—in fact, it's good business. Once you know what your options are, you can make your decisions accordingly. You can also—tactfully, of course—use a competitive offer to bargain.

Which brings us to money. You may or may not have discussed salary in the interview—career counselors suggest holding off and waiting until you've got an offer in hand—but through your research, you've probably got a general idea of what the starting salary range is for someone in your position. If you've been offered something at the high end, it might be best not to haggle. If what they're quoting is lower than you'd expect, now's the time to get down to business.

How to bargain for better wages? Keep the discussion as nonconfrontational as possible. Let your prospective employer know that you're flexible—you simply need more to live on—then give them a range of figures to work with. Finally, be candid about what you've been offered elsewhere—not in an aggressive way, but as an assertion of your worth. This entire back-and-forth thing really works only if you're serious about the job. Don't go through the hassle of getting your salary up if you're pretty sure you wouldn't take the position anyway. It's unnecessary and something of a bridge-burner.

> **Finding Out Starting Salary Ranges in Your Profession**
>
> - Ask contacts in the field.
> - Study the help-wanted ads for comparison.
> - Read trade journals and newsletters.
> - Consult reference books such as *The Occupational Outlook Handbook* or *The Jobs Rated Almanac.*
> - Ask at your college career center.

Should none of this yield an increase, consider a few alternatives to an immediate salary boost. Instead of money, you can ask for a three- or six-month salary review. This will let them know that you're going to be so valuable to the company that they'll want to give you a raise within just a few months. Or you might negotiate your vacation and/or starting dates. Come to the table in good faith and something will work out in your favor.

As soon as you've made your decision, get in touch with any other companies that you might be talking to and let them know of your plans. Don't wait on this one—you never know who'll be useful in your network in the future, and once you've made a connection, it's a good idea to keep it.

On the Job

There's some things even this book just can't teach you. How to tie a tie is one (too many diagrams . . . just go ask your dad already); how to enjoy wearing pantyhose is another (try calling them "stockings" . . . maybe that'll help). What we *really* can't advise you on, however, are all of the subtle and not-so-subtle rules, mores, and politics of your particular workplace. It'll take a couple of *months* to memorize the photocopier code, let alone such crucial office protocol as the amazingly complicated list of Who Likes E-mail/Who Likes Voicemail/Who Likes Paper; the all-important Names on the Memo hierarchy; the dreaded Must Stop and Chat at Their Cubicle checklist; and the brought-up-at-every-staff-meeting Who Is Leaving Crumbs in the Meeting Rooms? question. Figuring it all out is part of the joy (and agony) of being a newbie.

Sound terrifying? Don't worry! You can always consult the big bound booklet that magically appears in your cubicle a few days after you arrive. It's called "Workplace Guidelines," or "Employee Handbook," or something of the sort, and usually bears no resemblance to the actual "workplace" around you. However, it's fun to read in a hypothetical, in-case-of-a-water-landing-your-seat-cover-doubles-as-a-flotation-device sort of way.

Of course, there are a few guidelines we can offer that will apply to most work environments. The rest, as they say, is up to you.

Humility is a Virtue

"Great, so you have a college degree. Big fucking deal. New graduates have to realize they don't know anything yet, and learn to become part of the team."

—Employer

- **Don't be afraid to ask questions, especially in the beginning.** Some bosses and coworkers are better about letting you know how you're doing; some figure you'll get it worked out *someday* and leave you alone. Better to get feedback as often as you can—without annoying people. Which brings us to . . .

- **Try to get along with your coworkers.** Remember that point you made during your interview about being a "team player"? Now's the time to show it. Getting along with your peers and associates doesn't have to mean joining them every day after work for a drink, or eating lunch with them, or joining the gossip circles that inevitably spring up on the job. You can keep your own counsel, if you prefer, and still get along with the people you spend eight hours a day with. As we said earlier, work dynamics are, when it comes down to it, not so different from any other relationship dynamics you've probably encountered in your life. Being a fair, responsible, hardworking, and friendly person goes a long way to making your job easier. Chances are, you'll end up making a pal or two along the way. Nothing wrong with that . . . right?

- **Right. Just keep it platonic.** Office sex, no matter how much you try to avoid it, will leak out of whatever tidy "this is my personal life, this is my professional life" box you try to squeeze it into. What's more, stepped-up vigilance and enforcement of sexual harassment regulations makes the office possibly the *worst* place to look for a mate—especially among superiors and underlings.

- **Find a mentor.** Besides giving you the opportunity to learn by example, a mentor can also be an ally, providing you with interesting projects and greater responsibility. Your mentor could be your boss or someone from another department. Just remember—mentorship is a two-way street. As much as you rely on their guidance and protection, they rely on your allegiance and support. Treat the mentor-mentee relationship with respect and set up your boundaries early so that there's little chance for misunderstanding later on.

Listen, Grasshopper
"Those who seek mentoring will rule the great expanse under heaven." —Shu Ching, *Chinese Book of History*, c. 6th century B.C.

- **Be consistent.** This means being on time, returning people's phone calls, offering thanks when it's due, and staying at work until the job's done. The basics. But being consistent also has to do with knowing and respecting your limits—when you're young and on fire it seems like there's no way but up. That is, until you burn out from all those lunches at your desk (and breakfasts, and dinners), stressful deadlines, and general lack of sleep. Make sure that you're pacing yourself according to what you can do, feasibly, over a long period of time and your star will shine long past the time you leave the company.

It Just Ain't Right

For whatever reason, sometimes jobs just don't work out. There are any number of reasons why this might happen—so many, in fact, that I'm going to leave them up to your imagination and just cut to the chase. So you got laid off. Or fired. Or maybe you quit—"resigned," if you prefer. It's bound to happen sometime, and unless it becomes a pattern, you shouldn't waste your time worrying too much about it. (Some folks even say that being fired was the best thing that ever happened to them.)

In any case, if your job isn't working out—for whatever reason—it may be time to look for a new one. This isn't to say that you should quit at the first sign of trouble. As with a good friendship, seeing a job through the rocky times will eventually make it more meaningful to you. But if coming to work every day feels kind of like one long dentist appointment, we'd say some serious thinking is in order. It could be you just need a new job, in which case, dust off your resume (make sure to add your most recent job to it), consult chapter 10 again, and start looking.

Top Five Worst Jobs

Factoring in environment, stress, income, security, physical demands:

1. Roustabout/oil field laborer
2. Lumberjack
3. Fisherman
4. Construction worker
5. Cowboy

(Source: *The Jobs Rated Almanac*)

Or perhaps you're in need of a bigger life change. Something more fulfilling . . . challenging . . . personally enriching and deeply transformative. That or just, uh, different? If this is you—and you know who you are—just another J-O-B may not fill what you're hunkerin' for. In which case, read on for our suggestion on taking an alternate route.

CHAPTER 12

The Life of a Dot-Com

Ah, the dot-com dilemma. Should you join the modern-day wagon train out to Silicon Valley (or Silicon Alley in New York, or Austin, Texas, or one of any number of tech towns across the country), hoping to strike gold when you get there? Or should you take the slow and steady route and do the 9-to-5 thing until you figure out what you really want?

If you're a twentysomething, chances are you've given the whole dot-com thing a passing thought or two. Maybe you've even been offered a job . . . or taken one . . . or turned one down. Whatever your situation, if you've thought of becoming a "Net slave," as those in the business not-so-affectionately refer to themselves, this chapter may give you a heads-up on the realities of the digital existence.

Let's take the case of Ben, a software engineer recently graduated from the University of Michigan. Just after graduation, Ben was recruited by a well-known software company located in Chicago. Although there were boring days, he liked the job and earned about $50,000 a year for doing it. Not bad for right out of college, right? He especially liked the life he was starting to build for himself in Chicago.

After about a year at the old "brick-and-mortar" job, some friends from Michigan called Ben up. They had a great opportunity to do a healthcare start-up in Austin, Texas, and wanted him to join their team. It was pretty much the standard dot-com scenario: not much money to start off, but lots of stock options and the possibility of going public after a year or so of hard work—which could mean six figures and up for Ben and his friends. Problem was, the team from Michigan had to move fast to secure funding, so Ben had a weekend to decide. He e-mailed some of his friends and family, including this author, asking for advice. "Do I stay at the job I'm at," he wrote, "where I'm happy but a little bored? Or do I try to go bigger? Devote the next year-plus of my life to only this company? Live a life of a starving artist? Little play and all hard work . . . ."

He continued:

> I had a fantastic time in college, but I was one of few that was very much ready to close that chapter of my life. What do I do? I am 23. What's one year of my life, anyway? I fear that if I leave Chicago I am leaving a good thing—friends, parties, everything this place has to offer, plus my job, apartment, etc. And the funny way life works, I have a feeling that I will never make it back to this beautiful city.

Of course, like any good writer, I counseled him to take the road less traveled. It seemed exciting and promising, this dot-com world. Perfect for someone just starting out, the wind at his back, willing to take risks that may or may not pay off. My reply:

> The good news is, you're 23. And you're right . . . what's a year? So maybe the company fails and you are back to square one. Guess what? You can go right back to where you are now.

Money shouldn't be the lure, I argued. Instead, Ben's draw should be the opportunity to follow his heart, create something that he could call his own, and know that he was passionate enough about something to risk everything to get it. "Take as many risks as you can now," I wrote. "They will make all the difference to you later."

Ben didn't take the start-up job, after all, preferring a more secure path to one with lots of uncertainty and no guarantee of success. Turns out it was the right decision for the time. A few months later, in April 2000, the NASDAQ took a tumble, sending scores of dot-com companies into tailspins from which they never recovered.

Still, I stand by my words: *Follow your heart. It's what's truest.* If your heart's set on being a Web mogul with at least one IPO to your name, that's what you should do. Not for the money, and not because everyone else is doing it—those reasons dry up pretty quickly once you've spent fifteen hours of a day in a slapdash office with two coworkers, whom you may or may not like, and their *Star Wars* screensavers. Do it because you've got a vision and an entrepreneurial spirit, and because you know that even if you fail, you'll pick yourself back up and start all over. Do it because it's what you want. But know what you're getting into first. That's where we come in.

Silicon Valley or Bust

Reporter Patricia Nelson Limerick, writing for *The New York Times*, compared the dot-com phenomenon to the California Gold Rush of 1849. "Like the Internet boom," she wrote, "the California Gold Rush of 1849 was also a huge media event. It dominated national attention, and it fixed certain expectations in the American mindset: fortunes for the finding, riches waiting for men [and, we'd add, women] with the right pluck to come seize them." Silicon Valley: the land of chips and money. If you can just get there you're home-free.

Then came the NASDAQ meltdown, and heads began to roll. A new dot-com went belly up every week or so, and the ones that were left started changing their names. The appendage "dot-com" and a cute URL morphed back into monikers you could trust: Inc., Co., Group, and the like.

So are the dot-com days long gone? Certainly not. Sure, the craze might be over. (You know something's up when photocopied flyers start showing up around the neighborhood advertising get-rich-quick dot-com scams. One read: "If you can point and click, you can become the next dot-com success!!! Mentored by top Internet trainer! No obligation!" *Yeah, right*.) But the Internet is going to only get bigger, say analysts, and if you're committed to the Net and see it as not just a tool, but a different way of doing business altogether—well, hitch up your wagon, pardner . . . you're on the right track.

Who's Who Among Net Slaves

For a while it seemed like anyone affiliated with a dot-com was a millionaire. They were also all former computer geeks who spoke in code (HTML, XML, ASP, Flash, Java, Cold Fusion, whatever you prefer) and went to Trekkie conventions in their spare time. They all became rich in a matter of days (no one could figure out quite how), and if you just had a good enough idea (about what, we aren't sure), you, too, could be one of them.

It turns out even Silicon Valley has its proletariat. Here's an edited version of "The New Media Caste System," according to Bill Lessard and Steve Baldwin, the cocreators of the NetSlaves website (www.disobey.com/netslaves), a forum for digital workers and mouse jockeys around the world.

Mole People: Hackers, revolutionaries, and other weirdos who use the Internet to preach their causes

Social Workers: Those martyrs—e.g., "hosts" of online communities—who endure the endless stream of Net-based nonsense

Cybercops: People whose job it is to patrol chat rooms, discussion groups, and bulletin boards, looking for lurid material and for offensive people: pedophiles, stalkers, "mole people"

Cab Drivers: Roving new-media freelancers—designers, HTML coders, copywriters, beta-testers—whose bosses often skip out before paying their "fares"

Fry Cooks: Those who do the grunt work at deadline time, bearing the brunt of managerial tirades

Gold Diggers and Gigolos: The schmoozers, sycophants, and opportunistic philanderers who hold well-paying jobs, even though no one is quite sure what they do

Priests and Madmen: Influential journalists, analysts, and pundits who attempt to make sense of a sometimes shallow industry

(Source: Reprinted with permission from NetSlaves.com, 1998–2000, published by Disobey)

Dot-Com Myths vs. Dot-Com Realities

A few more myths that could stand some updating:

Myth: All dot-com companies (a) are located in sunny and beautiful Silicon Valley, California, and (b) do something called an IPO (initial public offering, i.e., putting your company on the stock market), which instantly makes everyone in the company a millionaire so that they never have to work again. This or they fail completely, in which case, everyone in the company goes broke and has to call their parents to send them tickets home to New Jersey.

Reality: A spring 2000 study by the accounting and consulting firm Ernst & Young paints a much less dramatic picture: a healthy two out of three Internet companies are making money, and half of that number claim to have no intention of going public. Also, more of the profitable online companies are located on the East Coast than in Silicon Valley. So there.

Myth: Everybody—except me—is becoming a millionaire!

Reality: The number of millionaires in America hasn't grown *that* much in recent years, despite stories of sudden dot-com wealth. Only about 4.5 percent a year since 1994—a steady, but not dramatic, rate according to market researchers at Claritas, Inc. That's because, as it turns out, people still tend to make money the old-fashioned way: by earning it. And a good way to earn it is by being an entrepreneur—dot-com or not. "Wealth is more often the result of a lifestyle of hard work, perseverance, planning, and, most of all, self-discipline," write Thomas Stanley and William Danko, authors of the book *The Millionaire Next Door* (Longstreet Press, 1996).

Myth: Putting up a website is fun and easy! A dash of HTML, a little Javascript, a DSL line here, a couple of programmers there . . . and presto-change-o! You're rich!

Reality: Are you *kidding*? The site itself is just the tip of the iceberg. Yes, you can do it cheaply, but know that the big guns usually pour in $750,000 or more when they bring a site to market. First, people have got to find the thing (out of the three trillion some-odd sites that are out there on the Web last time anybody checked). That means search services and marketing and advertising and word of mouth, just like a regular old brick-and-mortar company. Then of course there's the problem of technology: even big companies like eBay have glitches in their systems and phone lines that cause business outages of a day or more. And to make matters worse, there's the whole problem of *customers*. You've actually got to have a real business in there somewhere. Yikes!

Myth: People don't actually *work* at dot-com companies. No. They brainstorm. They meet with venture capitalists (VCs). They fly around the world with their wearable computers and laugh at the plebes thousands of miles below. When they actually have to be in the office, they get to drink beer, play video games and Nerf football in the meeting rooms, and surf the Internet.

Reality: Don't take it from me; take it from "sfdude@aol.com," writing on NetSlaves:

> Here we are on the front lines of the digital revolution. We are the young men and women who put in eighty-hour-plus work weeks to achieve fame and fortune on the glamorous frontier known as the Internet. We sacrifice family, friends, pets, and even plants for glorious stock options and home DSL connections. [Yet] when I talk to most of my friends over a three-dollar coffee at Starbucks, I get the general consensus that most of us are sort of stuck. We have SUV leases to pay. We're all striving to buy that one $400,000 condo that's being built in SF's Mission District. And don't forget about that month off that we plan to take in January to go to Australia. I'm not sure which January, or even if it will even happen this decade. I just know I'm going.

In reality, dot-commers are a lot less mysterious than you would think. They work just like everyone else—sometimes for longer hours, sometimes for better pay, though that isn't the rule. They aren't necessarily Trekkies or *Star Wars* fanatics, despite my earlier jokes, and they come in all shapes, colors, and sizes, just like people everywhere. Maybe they've got a bit more of the old entrepreneurial spirit in them than the regular Joe, but that's the American dream, after all.

Some Words of Advice

So if you're going to take the plunge—alone or with a dot-com organization, there are a few things you may want to keep in mind. Culled from industry sources, this is what folks say about how to run a dot-com business in the wake of the craze.

- Before you head out, ask yourself, "Why do I want to make the move?" Don't do it to make a quick buck. Do it because you're in it for the long haul—because you see the Internet as a better way of doing business.

- Think carefully about your business opportunity, your market, and your technological capabilities. But think hardest about the people with whom you're going to be working. What if your business takes off? The team you're building now should last you through both good times and bad. You're going to be spending a lot of time with these folks, so a sense of humor that matches your own wouldn't be a bad idea.

- Be comfortable with a certain amount of risk. One venture capital company says they read about 2,500 start-up business plans a year—and invest in only 25. That's a 1 percent chance of getting your business up and running if you don't already have funding. At the same time, as in the brick-and-mortar world, connections can increase your odds of getting your plan looked at—and possibly funded.

- Don't be a control freak. Even if your business is just you and your best friend from college, eventually (if the business is a success) you may want to hire someone, at which point you'll have to know how to delegate.

- You need more than hard work and technological knowledge to build a long-lasting business. You need passion and commitment as well as the belief that what you're doing actually matters to the world at large.

Of course, heading out to Silicon Valley is only one way to chart an alternate course for yourself, be an entrepreneur, and make a difference. There's yet another way to be a deeply fulfilled, independent, risk-taking, sleep-deprived, misunderstood genius *and* run the risk of never making a living—all at once. It's called being an artist.

CHAPTER 13

A Career in the Arts

A career in the arts. Try explaining *that* to your parents.

"But I can't be a humanitarian-aid-organization doctor, Mom. I'm too busy with my *performance art!*" Or, "Yes, I realize I told you I would take care of you in your old age, but I just don't think I want that $100,000-a-year investment banking job anymore. From now on, I'm putting my stock in *poetry!*" How about this one: "Dad, even though you risked your life to protect perfect strangers, I've realized the force just isn't for me. I've gotta . . . *dance!*"

If it sounds ridiculous, that's because it is . . . sort of. Being an artist—whether a painter, writer, videographer, rapper, whatever—isn't a career so much as it is a way of life; some people make money doing it, but lots don't. That's why art is art. There's no guarantee anyone is going to even *like* what you create, let alone pay money for it. Risk, uncertainty, hard work, passion, creation for its own sake—that's what makes art precious. And if art's your thing, nothing else will make you quite as happy or fulfill you quite as much as being able to practice your craft every day of every year for the rest of your life.

> ### Labor Pains
>
> "It's like being pregnant—you can read about it and think about it a lot, but nothing is going to prepare you for the experience of your first job except doing it. People think showbiz is a glamorous, exciting world, but in fact it's like that maybe twice a year. The rest of the time is full of hard, lugubrious work."
>
> —Television producer

Problem is, how do you do that *and* earn a living?

"Hi! My Name Is Todd, and I'll Be Your Waiter This Evening"

Everybody knows that all the waiters in L.A. are just actors waiting to be discovered. (In New York, they're writers. As the saying goes, "Throw a rock in any direction and chances are you'll hit one." Go ahead, put us out of our misery.) Every artist—well, okay, maybe not Britney Spears or the boys of 'N Sync, but their day will come—has had to do something other than their "art" to pay the bills. That's just the nature of the beast.

So you slog away, day after day . . . washing dishes, or telemarketing, or driving a cab, or waiting on tables, or walking dogs, or shelving books, or being someone's personal assistant, or proofreader, or phone sex operator (it's true!), or lifesize Disney character (true again!), or secretary, or bike messenger, or security guard, or maid.

And you wait, and wait, and wait . . . for your ship to come in, for a wealthy patron, for a sugar daddy, for a sugar mama, for a contract, for an agent, for an acceptance, for a nice rejection letter, for an audition, for a gallery to sign you, for a fellowship, for a grant, for a residency, for a teaching position, for a part, for a role, for a solo, *for your big break.*

> ### Not Quite the Full Monty
>
> **John Lavine** wanted to get into radio when he graduated from Boston University. "My *intention* was to buy a van and head across the country auditioning for radio stations until I found a job," John says. "I bought the van, but it was a lemon and broke down with a regularity that both astonished and pleased the repair shops of Boston." After spending all his money replacing virtually every component in the engine, he saw a classified ad for a deejay at the Naked i Cabaret. "I stood outside looking at this place with the flashing red lights, and thought, 'You really can't do this,' but I did. I auditioned, and got the job, and it paid the bills until I found a job in radio."

Unfortunately, your big break doesn't actually happen like it does in the movies. Or maybe it does, but those aren't the kind of movies you want to be in. (My, you've got a pretty face, Sally Jo! How would you like to come to Hollywood and be a *movie star*? First, we'd just like to get some test photographs of you. How about taking off your top?) *Noooo.* Big breaks are almost always the result of long years of lots and lots of hard work (the "break" is for backbreaking), practice, networking, and self-promotion—just like any other job. Or maybe even more than any other job, if you want to be successful at it.

Our point? Enter at your own risk. The arts are not for the fainthearted. But if you love what you do, it will all be worth it.

But How Do I Know If I'm an Artist?

If you've gotten this far in the chapter, chances are you're at least *interested.* Maybe you write short stories when you get home from work and secretly would love to see them published one day. Maybe you're happiest when you're painting and wish that you could find a way to do it more than on the one or two days every month when you're not too tired. Maybe you've hated every job you've ever had but are afraid to become an actor because your parents will think you're crazy. Or maybe not. Perhaps getting together with friends to play music occasionally is enough to satisfy your creative urges. Or you're a weekend watercolorist, or a once-a-summer community theatre player. Remember: There are lots of ways of being an artist—making a career of it is just one of them.

So take a little while to think about who you are, what you want from your art, and what you envision for your life. Julia Cameron's book, *The Artist's Way: A Spiritual Path to Higher Creativity* (J.P. Tarcher, 1992), as well as Anne Lamott's *Bird by Bird: Some Instructions on Writing and Life* (Anchor, 1995), can help you to sort out some of the reasons why you may or may not want to write, paint, play music, be a photographer, etc. Making the decision of whether or not to pursue a career in the arts can take years—in many cases, even a lifetime—so go easy on yourself. Save the self-flagellation for later . . . when you've figured out what you want to do. You'll need it as motivation to go on the week's fifteenth audition . . . send out your novel for the twenty-seventh time . . . play at yet another bar mitzvah.

Makin' It

Unfortunately, being talented, motivated, committed, passionate, brave, a visionary, and a little bit nuts *alone* won't make you a star. (To tell you the truth, it won't even buy you a box of ninety-nine-cent macaroni and cheese, let alone pay your rent or keep you in oil paints, film, toe shoes, ripped sweatshirts, smearable chocolate, or whatever it is you need to do what you do.) To have an actual *career* in the arts, i.e., to make money performing, dancing, writing, singing, painting, etc., you've got do what folks in every job do. That is, (1) have a plan, (2) network, (3) sell yourself, (4) hit the pavement, and (5) repeat numbers one through four as many times as necessary.

That's right . . . being an artiste doesn't exempt you from needing some business sense. In fact, you've got to be even more savvy—especially in things like self-promotion, finances (including taxes and insurance), and networking. Who else but you is going to watch your bottom line? This is even more important as you get older and, we hope, more successful. Money has a way of attracting lots of shady characters claiming to have your best interests in mind. Best you keep track of your *own* enterprise from the beginning. We have some tips to help you get started.

Have a Plan

Besides the whole "Am I an artist?" thing, there are many questions you need to ask yourself as you're starting out on your career. Do you want to work in the fine (painter, sculptor, novelist, etc.) or applied arts (furniture-maker, graphic designer, copywriter)? Or would you be comfortable doing both? What about the whole M.F.A. (Master of Fine Arts) thing? Should you go back to school, knowing that while it may deepen your craft and open up some doors, it may also put you deep into debt? Speaking of debt, how much are you willing to handle as you get your career off the ground? Unless you're independently wealthy, if you have zero tolerance for debt you're going to want to live in a place where you can just scrape by—not New York City or San Francisco or Paris or any number of "artsy" expensive cities. And how about work? Would you rather do something akin to your art so you can get your foot in the door, or should you work at a totally unrelated job (poet Thom Lux suggests security guard) so that you have time to think and you can save all your energy for your own stuff? Another question: Are you willing to teach in your discipline, knowing that teaching can sometimes sap young artists of their creative juices?

> ## The Big Break(-In)
>
> **Jenny Horst** majored in theater at Wesleyan. After she graduated, she came to New York to find a job in the theater. A friend of a friend suggested she call the theatrical producer Jed Feuer. He invited her to come to his apartment for an interview (this sort of thing happens in the theater). When she rang his buzzer, he came out to the front door of the building to let her in, and the door to his apartment slammed shut. "I'm standing in the hallway with this producer in his socks, and he's locked out of his apartment," Jenny remembers. So, she took out a credit card and burgled his front door. Did she get the job? Are you kidding?

Then, of course, there's the whole matter of work, discipline, and practice. When, where, how? *When:* We are creatures of habit; finding a time to sit down and do your work every day transforms your art from hobby to profession. *Where:* Must you have a studio? Or will a large closet suffice? If you're a photographer and you don't have a darkroom, you'll need to arrange your life so that you're near one. *How:* Are you, like writer Graham Greene, a 500-words-a-day type, or do you work in fits and starts? Do you need people and culture around you, or are you happy to work in relative isolation—a latter-day Thoreau on his pond?

Finally, what about the long term? What projects/books/paintings/performances do you have in your mind to keep you motivated during the dark days (and every artist has them)? What about basic stuff like getting paid, invoices, and health insurance—not to mention agents, investments, retirement money, taxes? Even artists have to answer to the IRS. (Consider hiring a good, reputable accountant who specializes in artist-types if you can't deal with your finances yourself.) Having a plan to deal with the big conceptual "what am I trying to say" issues as well as the picayune details of everyday life will help you stay focused and confident—and paid, let's not forget that—as you head into the world.

Network

The same stuff we said in chapter 9 applies here—maybe even more so, as artists have a tendency to isolate themselves. "Lonely writer/painter/musician" and all that jazz. Truth is, artists need a community, too, so they can share their ideas, seek out mentors and peers to collaborate with, have their work critiqued and praised, challenge themselves, and find support for what they do.

Networking in the art world works pretty much the same way it does anywhere—through school, work, and professional organizations, as well as through personal connections and mentoring relationships. Because of the competitive nature of the work, however, and the general lack of money for most things we call artistic, things like access to M.F.A. programs, fellowships, grants, and artists' colonies—let alone actual jobs/contracts/assignments—is often limited to the proverbial "who knows whom." Add to that the need for agents and artists' representatives, and you can imagine the amount of, shall we say . . . butt-kissing? . . . that goes on out there. That doesn't mean you've got to kneel down with the rest of them. As in other professions, honesty, integrity, and real talent will get you everywhere. Being a sycophantic busybody will get you a couple of hors d'oeuvres at a cocktail party. At the same time, keeping in touch with folks in your network is crucial if you want to make a career of your art.

Again, as in other industries, broaden your reach by keeping track of what's going on in your field. Read the trade papers and magazines (*Variety* for folks in the film industry, *Poets & Writers* for literary types, *Communication Arts* for designers, etc.). Look on the Web for discussion groups and resource sites. Attend functions—those readings, gallery openings, dance performances, etc., don't have to be expensive. If there's a union, join it (Screen Actors Guild [SAG], National Writers Union). Just remember not to fill your schedule up with "networking" (read: social) functions. There's a difference between *saying* at a party that you're a writer/muralist/salsa dancer/rock-and-roll musician and actually *being* one. Being one means you go home after the party (or at least wake up the next morning) and work on your art. There ain't no other way around it.

> ### Pennies for Your Thoughts
> The National Writers Union accepts members in three levels: first level earning under $5,000; second level earning from $5,000 to $25,000; third level earning from $25,000 on up. "The vast majority" of members are in the first level, according to Marty Waldman, of the NWU.

Sell Yourself

Not literally, though I do know of a mild-mannered writer by day who doubles as an Internet porn star by night. . . .

Selling yourself is the same thing as *marketing yourself*, which is the same thing as *putting together a good package*, which is the same thing as *getting your act together*. All different names for the same basic concept: looking and acting like the smart, capable, confident, fabulously creative person that you are.

How to do it? Well, first you've got to know what you're selling and to whom. Are you a nonfiction writer who has a great idea for a book? Pick up a guide to writing books at your local bookstore and tap into your network to see if there are any agents/professors/mentor types who will help shepherd your idea to completion. Or maybe you're a graphic designer who wants to get into advertising. You've got examples of your work, but no one to whom you can show it. Why not put together a website featuring all of your masterpieces, then send out a catchy mailing with your URL address to your top ten favorite ad firms and see who bites?

In general, a well-designed image helps get the message across to those who are dispensing the cash that you are a professional and that you should be treated (and compensated) as such. Whatever your discipline, consider developing an integrated promotional package for yourself that includes:

- A resume/CV that lists your education, professional accomplishments, artistic achievements, and any grants, fellowships, or awards you've received for your work

- Simple letterhead/envelopes for professional correspondence (like cover and thank-you letters, applications, follow-up notes, and invoices)

- A business card (so you don't have to write your name down on napkins anymore)

- Samples of your best work (writing or film clips, slides, videos of performances, etc.), packaged nicely

- A personal website where you can house an online version of your contact information, professional qualifications, portfolio/clips, and any other information about you and your work that would be relevant to the public (performance schedules, gigs you've played, links, book lists, works you have for sale, etc.)

It doesn't have to be fancy or full of bells and whistles. It should, however, present your work in a clear, confident manner. That way, when you're at your next party/networking event/interview, or when you're applying for your next grant/residency/job, you have ways for people interested in your work to follow through and find out more.

Hit the Pavement

In other words, you actually have to use all this nice promotional stuff you're developing for yourself to *get work*. Oddly enough, for many artists just starting out, the aspect that scares them most isn't the instability, the risk, the night after night of ramen for dinner . . . it's the possibility of *getting paid* for doing what they supposedly love to do. Perhaps it's fear of actually having to perform for someone instead of in front of the mirror; perhaps it's a lack of faith in one's own talent; perhaps it's a desire to remain untainted by the demon dollar. None of these is a good reason. Fear of success has kept many a good artist down— but not you. Repeat after me: *I want to get paid for doing what I love to do. That will allow me to quit my stupid day job and devote myself entirely to my macaroni art* (or whatever else it is you do). *I will improve and grow and eventually join the ranks of such one-named luminaries as Shakespeare, Michelangelo, Picasso, Ellington, Hendrix, and Madonna.*

So get out there! Look for books on ways to crack the business. Hire yourself out for odd jobs as well as freelance and temp assignments in your industry so that you can get your foot in the door and make connections. Rifle through the online sites. Call the folks in your network and see if there's anyone out there willing to hire you to do what you want to do. Apply for every grant, residency, and fellowship for which you're eligible. (Consult the Foundation Center, www.fdncenter.org, for more information on finding funding, as well as any number of books on scholarships, grants, and residencies for artists at your local bookstore.) Send that poem out a hundred times, or until it gets published. Pitch your screenplays to every studio you can find. Every bit of work you do now to get your career up and running will make a difference in the long run. And in the meantime, try to make your paying job one that pays well and takes as little time and energy as possible, so that you can work on your own stuff on the side.

> ### It's Who You Know
>
> **Jonathan Arak** really wanted to direct. At Oberlin, he checked out the career placement center, but "they didn't really have any job leads in theater," Jonathan explains. "They had a lot of information about graduate programs, but I didn't want to spend three years and another $60,000 to arrive in New York with an M.F.A. and be on the same rung of the ladder as everyone else anyway."
>
> Jonathan decided to write a Great Letter. He sent one copy to Harold Prince, one to Roundabout Theater, and one to the Circle Repertory Company. "It really was a great letter talking about things I'd done at school, but it turned out the most important thing was that I mentioned was that John Kander, who wrote the music for *Cabaret* and *New York, New York,* had seen my production of *Company* back at Oberlin and had been very impressed.
>
> "Well, Hal Prince actually called Kander, who waxed poetic about me on the phone for half an hour, so Hal Prince hired me. I've been assistant to the director for his productions of *Don Giovanni* at New York City Opera, the first version of *Kiss of the Spiderwoman* in Purchase, New York, *The Grandchild of Kings* off-Broadway, and I will be stage managing *Kiss of the Spiderwoman* when it comes to Broadway later this year."

Success may come slowly, but it will come. Work on your art, educate yourself, and develop your network in the meantime. Then, once you've sold that painting, written that book, covered that building with a supersize condom at the taxpayers' expense, you can . . .

Repeat Numbers One Through Four Again

Why? Because it's your life *and* your job, and because an artist's work is never done.

Advice from the Trenches

So get out there and do your thing. Now's as good a time as any. But why take our word for it? Here's what the artists—and the people who work with them— have to say.

Kirk Smith, vice president, Starr Seigle Communications

Like a lot of work, some of the very best training for artists is "on the job." Get to know the people whom you would like to work with by providing them what they need, whatever that may be. Most of the people I know who successfully work in a creative or artistic field got there by literally sweeping the floors, carrying out the trash, and just being around at the right time. There are more careers made on timing than all the casting calls, auditions, and artist contests put together. The successful creative people I have known would do anything just to be around their art, and their ability to succeed was more determination than talent. Creative work is far different than just being creative and it is usually never limited to just one discipline because it involves people who bring that creativity to everything they do.

Nancy Agabian, performer and writer

Get a no- or low-stress job where you don't have to think. Don't waste your creative energy at a job where you are contributing to someone else's dream— save it for your own art. Make only enough money to survive and buy art supplies, costumes, books, whatever your medium is. Don't wait to be an artist! Your early twenties are the only time in your life when it is socially acceptable to just scrape by financially, and when all your other friends will be in similar poverty-stricken positions. Look into part-time jobs that pay a decent wage. For the first four years out of college I worked as an artist's assistant. It paid pretty well and I only worked four days a week. Over the years, I had enough time to write, do readings around town, and develop performances. I slowly gained a following for my work, enough so that I was eventually able to support myself through teaching workshops. Give yourself the permission to start small and grow over the years. You're young! You don't have to be good at anything yet!

Isabel Chang, Web designer/artist

Find one thing you know a lot about and kick ass with it.

Samantha Schnee, editor

Go into a big-money job for three or four years and view it as indentured servitude. Save up a whole ton of money and then launch the arts career when there's enough moola in the coffers to support yourself. The problem is that at some point it runs out, but, hey, then you can always go into credit card debt, right?

Jana Ragsdale, assistant dean, Columbia University School of the Arts

From where I sit, I'd say that you shouldn't apply to grad school until you've actually done something in your field. Working in a gallery/as an author's assistant/ etc. can be extremely informative in the early stages of your career. Knowing how the business of the arts operates helps you to understand what you need besides raw talent to get there. Just don't do it for too long: you risk becoming either jaded or known only as Joe, "the assistant for _____ Gallery," or Jane, "famous author's lackey."

As for style, if you are a poor and starving artist you can dress funky in thrift store cheap, but always have nice shoes. And no matter what field you are in, always send a thank-you note the very next day to anyone who has done anything for you: fed you, made a connection for you, etc.

Barbara Seaman, writer

Finding the right mentors may count more than finding the right jobs or schools. After 40 years of intimate observation in book and magazine publishing (I'm an author and journalist, but I've also worked as an in-house or contributing editor at eight distinct magazines), I've perceived there are two fundamental styles of "managers" out there: those who train a staffer or assistant and strive to keep her or him "in place"—not unkindly, necessarily, but for efficiency's sake; and those who count among their finest achievements in life the young people they trained up and set aloft. When aspiring writers or editors say to me, "So how is it to work at *Ladies' Home Journal* magazine or William Morrow book publishers?" I answer with such questions as "Which department? What editor?"

They say that to get published or get ahead in publishing, it's not what you know but whom you know. That's not untrue, but more to the point is who knows *you*— who recognizes your genius or talent, and who is willing to go to bat for you.

J. H. Carroll, journalist

Journalists, take note: If you've ever felt like you've mastered the intricacies of a complicated topic—foreign debt valuation, Rwandan intertribal tension, the revival of capri pants—only to receive eleven column inches (or even worse, a mere hyperlinked blurb) in return for your toil, then consider going the route of the TV game show. It's the sweetest revenge. All those factoids you accumulated freelancing for some rarely read community newspaper can now be put to lucrative use. So what if the editor deleted that parenthetical detail about Edward the Confessor's crest? If you blurt it before the buzzer, valuable cash and prizes (and home-version board games) will be yours. And there's no better time to make a buck off trivia than the present: prime-time powerhouses like *Who Wants to Be a Millionaire, Twenty-One,* and *Greed* are awaiting your wisdom, and for those who prefer an actual challenge, there's always *Jeopardy!* So go for it. Your parents will be ecstatic you didn't hit them up for money. And, they will get to watch you not doing it.

Duscha Gretel Zellerhoff, filmmaker

I started to make money by collecting bottles on the beach. . . .

As a young filmmaker it's necessary to be without money for a while. Don't worry about it. You can work in several professions. Later, when you are a famous director, you can order everyone around (including the people you used to work for).

Or you can collect bottles on the beach, find a dead body instead, and then you'll have your first screenplay!

Eden Elieff, writer

Find a core of artists whose sensibilities speak to yours, that can serve as a model to yours. Surround yourself with their work, or if you're lucky, develop contact with them so you can learn as much as you can from them. If that means going to school where they teach, do so. If that means finding a way to correspond with them, do so. During the long process of artistic development, you'll need the inspiration of their example. And I define inspiration as a feeling of possibility. When times get tough, you need to summon work that tells you that your own vision and impulse can achieve expression.

Karina Livingston, teacher and youth advocate

I have always been impressed with people who publish their own stuff. A friend of mine, Libby, puts out a publication called *Grow Your Own 'Zine* and has gotten quite a following by just doing it. Now she is in a compilation of best 'zines. So, don't be afraid to call it art and put it out there.

CHAPTER 14

Putting It Off

Putting it off. What's that supposed to mean? "Doing nothing" after graduation isn't really an option, is it? Whether you're living at home or out on your own or traveling around the world, if you're a living, breathing, thinking human being, you're doing *something*. (Brushing your teeth counts. So does hanging out in a hammock in Phuket. Ditto *Oprah;* ditto partying with your friends.) Preferably, however, you'll want to spend these first few years after college doing something that educates and challenges you, expands your horizons, and allows you to do some thinking about yourself and your life goals.

Happily, this does not mean you have to immediately start working full time at a traditional job that fits neatly into your long-range career plans. (Of course if you do have it all figured out at the age of twenty-one, well . . . bully for you! The rest of us mere mortals need a couple of years to catch up.) You can be a bit lost—even unfocused, misdirected, confused, and perplexed—and still have valuable, important, life-changing post-college experiences. In fact, we'd say that letting yourself dangle around for a little while when you're relatively young and flexible might save you a midlife crisis or two later. No guarantees, of course. What you make out of these next couple of years is strictly up to you. Remember: We're all works-in-progress; "putting it off" is just another way to say "figuring it out." And for most of us, that takes a lifetime.

Yeah, yeah . . . but what do I do right now?

Taking Time Off

Sometimes, all you need to get focused and "back on track," as parent-types like to say, is time, pure and simple. Maybe you're burned out from school. Maybe you've got some idea of what you'd like to do next, but you're not quite ready, or you're unsure of what your first step should be. If this is the case, consider just taking a few months to get yourself physically, emotionally, and mentally rested before you head back out into the world again. If you're supporting yourself, get a job you're at least vaguely interested in and consider it an investment in your future. If you can mooch off your parents for a while, do. As we mentioned in the introduction to this book, a few months with the folks will most likely provide enough incentive for you to move back out on your own pretty quickly.

Whichever route you take, make sure to spend at least some of your time thinking about what you want, exploring your options, scanning the classifieds, and developing your network. That way, when you're ready to emerge from your cave (or is that a chrysalis?), you'll have a few leads to follow and some folks to help guide you.

Working Abroad

Nineteenth-century Europeans used to call it *wunderjahr*—from which you returned philosophically expanded and emotionally refreshed, ready to take on the responsibilities of the adult world. Denizens of the new millennium just call it "traveling"—or, in Australia, "trekking"—and there are thousands and thousands of twentysomethings all over the world who are having quite a lot of fun (and maybe even expanding their souls a centimeter or two) while drifting hither and thither across the globe in search of a new adventure and yet another cheap hostel.

In fact, it's pretty much required for Scandinavians, Aussies, and New Zealanders of a certain age (and socioeconomic status, may we add) to spend a year or two working and traveling their way around the world. What possesses them to leave behind friends and family, home and security, clean beds and potable water for the busy streets of Bangkok or the jungles of the Amazon? Sometimes it's simple: you just need a break from the grind . . . a getaway . . . an adventure. And sometimes the reasons for traveling run deeper. It's true that the farther you get from home, the clearer your perspective becomes. Seeing how the rest of the world lives makes you appreciate your own relative comfort, wealth, opportunity, and freedom. It's a life-changing experience to meet people from faraway places who may have different ideas about the way the world works—and yet who are willing to share a few moments, or a dinner, or even their homes with you. At the very least, it opens you up to something called *humanity*.

Fortunately, if you're short on dough, there are ways to travel *and* work at the same time (teaching English, organic farming, being a nanny or an au pair), and several books can help guide your search. Try one or all of the following:

- Vacation Work's *Work Your Way Around the World* (9th edition) by Susan Griffith (Petersons Guides, 1999)

- *Teaching English Abroad: Talk Your Way Around the World!* (4th edition) by Susan Griffith (Vacation Work, 1999)

- *Work Abroad: The Complete Guide to Finding a Job Overseas* edited by Clayton A. Hubbs (Transitions Abroad, 1999)

- *How to Get a Job in Europe* (4th edition) by Robert Sanborn and Cheryl Matherly (Surrey Books, 1999)

- *International Jobs: Where They Are, How to Get Them* (5th edition) by Eric Kocher and Nina Segal (Perseus, 1999)

In addition, *O-Hayo Sensei* (www.ohayosensei.com) is a free, twice-monthly newsletter that researches and lists currently available teaching (and other English language–related) positions. When you're ready to make your arrangements, try to finagle yourself an International Student Identity Card, as well as an International Youth Hostel (IYH) membership, both of which can save you *beaucoup* bucks on everything from train tickets to sleeping accommodations to Internet café rentals. If you're going to be on the road for more than a few months, we suggest preparing yourself by reading a few books—historical and literary—about the places you'll be visiting. And a general "travelers on traveling" collection may be worth your time, too—Rough Guides publishes a great compendium of travel essays for women called *More Women Travel: Adventures and Advice from More Than 60 Countries* edited by Natania Jansz and Miranda Davies (Rough Guides, 1995) and *Travelers' Tales: A Woman's World* edited by Marybeth Bond (Traveler's Tales, 1995). The magazine *Transitions Abroad* also has monthly updates on jobs, schools, and programs overseas, as well as travelers' tips, stories, and guides to destinations well off the Frommer's path.

Of course, you don't have to leave the country to go abroad. For those who want to stick a little closer to home, there's always that post-college rite of passage, the cross-country road trip. (Yes, the Grand Tetons do look like breasts, just like those French settlers said.) Or should you want to extend your travels into a couple of months of work here and there, *The Back Door Guide to Short Term Job Adventures: Internships, Extraordinary Experiences, Seasonal Jobs, Volunteering, Work Abroad* by Michael Landes (Ten Speed Press, 1997) gives you the lowdown on everything from salmon fishing in Alaska (tons o' cash but you have to sleep in shifts) to ski-bumming in Vail (dude!) to being a forest ranger at Hawaii's Volcanoes National Park.

Good Works

If you can spare the time and energy, and if you can afford to live on the cheap for a few months—or years—consider working in the not-for-profit/volunteer sector for a while. You won't necessarily make a ton, but you'll have the benefit of knowing that your work directly touches people's lives—not something you're guaranteed in your basic corporate gig.

Since the early 1990s, nationwide service organizations like City Year (www.cityyear.org) and Americorps (www.americorps.org) have been recruiting young people to help make a difference in communities around the United States. Not only do program participants gain work experience, but they are also usually awarded a small stipend (enough to live on), earn healthcare and childcare benefits, and receive educational grants once they have completed their year of work.

Another option is Teach for America (www.teachforamerica.org), a program designed to attract bright, motivated young people just out of college (but without a teaching certificate) back into the public schools. Teachers spend two years working in schools around the country—some urban, some rural—and in return receive teacher training and certification, a yearly salary and benefits, and the chance to make a difference in a few children's lives. The application process is competitive and somewhat lengthy. Call 800-832-1230 in the fall of your senior year for more information.

So I Did This Mission Thing . . .

"They'd better have a damn good reason."

—Investment banker, talking about suspicious holes in resumes

Finally, besides the granddaddy of all service organizations—the Peace Corps, scaled back somewhat since its heyday during the late 1960s and 1970s (contact them at www.peacecorps.com or 800-424-8580 for an application and information)—there are many local, nationwide, and even worldwide not-for-profit and volunteer entities just waiting for folks like you to offer your help, hope, and optimism—for instance, Habitat for Humanity, the Jesuit Volunteer Corps, and the Friends' Service Committee, just to name a few. Many more jobs, organizations, and volunteer opportunities can be found in the following books:

- *The International Directory of Voluntary Work* (7th edition) by Louise Whetter and Victoria Pybus (Vacation Work, 2000)

- *Volunteer America: A Comprehensive National Guide to Opportunities for Service, Training, and Work Experience* by Harriet Clyde Kipps (Ferguson Publishing, 1997)

- *Volunteering: 101 Ways You Can Improve the World and Your Life* by Douglas M. Lawson (1998)

Graduate School

Far be it from us to pooh-pooh the life of the mind. And let's face it—grad school is quickly becoming the standard for professionals beyond the traditional fields of medicine, law, science, and academia. So, if you're dying to start your work in biochemical engineering or copyright law or Roman bathing rituals or nineteenth-century English eating habits as represented in the works of Jane Austen . . . well, then . . . hop to it! (If it's you I've just described, you're probably already writing your doctoral thesis and are reading this book because you're some kind of techno-anthropologist studying post-postmodern early-twenty-first-century Internet-induced career and life angst . . . or something. If so, we pity you.)

Or maybe you've thought about grad school, but in a sort of hazy wouldn't-it-be-nice-to-study-in-the-library-again way—like most of us who applied to grad school right out of college in a desperate attempt to stave off real life.

Doing What's Necessary

Doug McMullen has published a couple of short stories since he finished college. However, since most of the prestigious literary magazines pay only about $250 a story, Doug has been forced to support himself in other ways. Here are some of the things he has done to pay the rent: photographed people dressed up in Edwardian costume on top of the Empire State Building; cut wildflowers in fields in upstate New York, drove back to the city, and sold them to florists; worked for a photographer hand-tinting flesh tones on cherubs for fake nineteenth-century lithographs; operated spotlights for a circus; survived as a bike messenger; acted as chauffeur for a Japanese Kyogen group (like Kabuki); worked as a puppeteer; and toiled as a bouncer—all of this in a two-year period.

Sorry to be such a buzzkill, but unless you know what you want to do in grad school ("learn" is not an adequate response), don't waste your money. Save it for when you *do* know exactly what you want to pursue, and then luxuriously enjoy one, two, or three (or seven!) years of student life when you're far enough away from college to really enjoy them. In the meantime, get a life, get a job, and study up on which schools you may want to attend should you ever decide to go back. (Not to mention preparing for your GREs, which ask you to remember things like "hypotenuse" and "quadratic equation." What *are* those?) There are quite a few books to help you in your quest:

- *Getting What You Came For: The Smart Student's Guide to Earning a Master's or a Ph.D.* by Robert L. Peters (Noonday Press, 1997)

- *Complete Book of Medical Schools* by Malaika Stoll (Princeton Review, 2001)

- *Complete Book of Business Schools* by Nedda Gilbert (Princeton Review, 2001)

- *Complete Book of Law Schools* by Eric Owens (Princeton Review, 2001)

You're on Your Own, Kid

So. You've gotten to the end of this book. Made it through all of the self-analysis, the corny jokes, and the boring stuff about how to find insurance. You've read so many "helpful hints" you feel like you could start a column of your own. Maybe you've laughed a little. Maybe you've cried. Maybe it was better than *Cats!* And yet, as you come to this very last chapter, you believe that it's all been worth it, for you've realized something very important about yourself:

You *still* have no idea what you want to do with your life.

Should you become a doctor? Move to Mexico? Join the military? The Hare Krishnas? The cast of *The Real World? Survivor?* Is graduate school the way to go? Is Australia? Or should you just give it all up and crawl back home to Mom and Dad?

Perhaps, but don't tell them *we* said so. In other words, whatever you do right now—whether it's work, or travel, or hanging around your old hometown reading poetry and cruising the mall—is okay, because sooner or later you're going to figure out what it is you really want to be doing and start doing it. Of course, that's as long as you stay open and attentive to where you are and what you want for yourself. Hopefully, this book has given you some of the practical skills you'll need to make it through these next few years with confidence, independence, style, and grace (and without too much debt). Hopefully, too, it has made you ask yourself a few questions about the kind of person you are and what you want for the future.

We've tried to help you make the process of living on your own (remember: *process,* not *destination*) a little less frustrating than it can be when you have to make the mistakes yourself. But you inevitably will make mistakes. Don't beat yourself up when you do. Chalk up any losses as the cost of an Education of Life—something you definitely *can't* pay for with your Visa.

About the Author

A resident of New York City by way of Hawaii, New Hampshire, Oregon, and Chicago, Tara Bray is a graduate of Dartmouth College as well as Columbia University's School of the Arts. When she's not writing, Tara likes to spend her time figuring out how to pay the rent. This is her first book.

Notes

Notes

Notes

Notes

Notes

Notes

Notes

Notes

Notes

Notes

Notes

Notes

Expert Advice

www.review.com

Talk About It

www.review.com

Pop Surveys

Paying for it

www.review.com

The Princeton Review

www.review.com

Getting in

Word du Jour

www.review.com

Find-O-Rama School & Career Search

www.review.com

Best Schools

Finding it

www.review.com

FIND US...

International

Hong Kong
4/F Sun Hung Kai Centre
30 Harbour Road, Wan Chai,
Hong Kong
Tel: (011)85-2-517-3016

Japan
Fuji Building 40, 15-14
Sakuragaokacho, Shibuya Ku,
Tokyo 150, Japan
Tel: (011)81-3-3463-1343

Korea
Tae Young Bldg, 944-24,
Daechi- Dong, Kangnam-Ku
The Princeton Review- ANC
Seoul, Korea 135-280,
South Korea
Tel: (011)82-2-554-7763

Mexico City
PR Mex S De RL De Cv
Guanajuato 228 Col. Roma
06700 Mexico D.F., Mexico
Tel: 525-564-9468

Montreal
666 Sherbrooke St.
West, Suite 202
Montreal, QC H3A 1E7 Canada
Tel: (514) 499-0870

Pakistan
1 Bawa Park - 90 Upper Mall
Lahore, Pakistan
Tel: (011)92-42-571-2315

Spain
Pza. Castilla, 3 - 5° A, 28046
Madrid, Spain
Tel: (011)341-323-4212

Taiwan
155 Chung Hsiao East Road
Section 4 - 4th Floor,
Taipei R.O.C., Taiwan
Tel: (011)886-2-751-1243

Thailand
Building One, 99 Wireless Road
Bangkok, Thailand 10330
Tel: (662) 256-7080

Toronto
1240 Bay Street, Suite 300
Toronto M5R 2A7 Canada
Tel: (800) 495-7737
Tel: (716) 839-4391

locations

National (U.S.)
We have over 60 offices around the United States and
run courses in over 400 sites. For courses and locations
within the U.S. call 1 (800) 2. Review and you will be
routed to the nearest office.